Shakespeare On Spirituality

Copyright © 2003 Craig Stephans
All rights reserved.
ISBN: 1-59457-146-5

To order additional copies, please contact us.
BookSurge, LLC
www.booksurge.com
1-866-308-6235
orders@booksurge.com

CRAIG STEPHANS

Shakespeare On Spirituality

Life-Changing Wisdom from
Shakespeare's Plays

2003

Shakespeare On Spirituality

For Madeline Emerson Stephans, that she may love Shakespeare and live spiritually

CONTENTS

Contents	
Acknowledgements	ix
Introduction	xi
Action—The Fruit of Spirituality	1
Angels Everywhere	5
Appearances Can be Deceiving	9
Approval from People Comes and Goes	17
Attitude, Attitude, Attitude	21
Character Matters	25
A Cheerful Heart	29
Contentment Above All Things	31
Death—Heaven or Hell	35
Demons and Witches	45
Depression and Despair: Enemies Within	51
Divine Rights of All	57
Drunkenness Leads to Stumbling	63
Evil Nature of Humans	67
Fear Less	79
Friendships Make Life Worth Living	83
Grief: A Necessary Part of Life	89
Guilt: Just Say No!	95
Individual Responsibility: Please Take It	101
Intuition: the Spirit's Voice	105
Love of All	109
Loyalty is Priceless	115
Marriage Vows	123
Mercy Me	131
Prayer Changes Everything	137
Pride Comes before a Fall	141

Providence along the Way	147
Reformation of the Soul	149
Repentance of Sin	157
Sin—Warning	163
Spiritual Battles	171
Stealing Religion	177
Vanity, Vanity	183
Virtue of Virtues	189

ACKNOWLEDGEMENTS

Thanks to Jerry and Billie Bacon for their continued support and encouragement for my writing. Thanks to Mike Stephans for his encouragement for each new endeavor. I am grateful to Missy and Madeline Stephans for their patience and understanding. For the original artwork—*Hamlet Act I*, featured on the cover, thanks to my friend and fellow writer James-Jason Gantt, author of the novel *Losing Summer.* Finally, Thanks to God for all of the good things I have enjoyed during my life.

INTRODUCTION

In Shakespeare's play *Julius Caesar,* following Caesar's murder by the conspirators, Marc Antony inspires the crowd of Romans as he declares to them, "I only speak right on; I tell you that which you yourselves do know." (Act III, scene ii) Like the effect Antony's words have on his hearers, Shakespeare's plays enlighten our minds to the truths that we know in our hearts. He brings them to our consciousness; he presents life—the essence of life—before our eyes. I believe the tremendous value of the plays is due to their foundation in truth—eternal truth.

This is why I have culled the plays to present Shakespeare's insights into spirituality and life. I believe they teem with lessons that we can apply in our lives.

For the purpose of my book, I define spirituality as the relationships we have with God, other people, ourselves and with the world. I include topics that affect these relationships and that Shakespeare addresses in his plays. His works offer myriad spiritual truths, lessons, and guidelines for life.

I have written this book to appeal to readers who have an interest in spirituality, personal development or, of course, in Shakespeare.

Although Shakespeare's writing lends itself to comparisons directly to the Bible, mythology or other religious and historical texts, I do not point out such comparisons in this book. I focus on the ideas and lessons Shakespeare presents, so that readers can draw their own conclusions about the relation of Shakespeare's writings to beliefs of particular religions. No matter what religious beliefs and background someone might have, this book offers meaningful spiritual insights about life.

I found that the several available variations of Shakespeare's texts have only minor differences, usually in spelling or punctuation. For the Shakespeare quotes in this book, I primarily use text from the *Shakespeare Head* edition of the plays. This is the version used in *The Complete Works of William Shakespeare* published by Barnes and Noble.

Researching and writing this book was an adventure for me. I felt like I was on a treasure hunt, discovering one gem after another. The plays are mines in which a person can spend a lifetime searching in a literary mother lode. I have no doubt that this book covers only a fraction of what could be written about spirituality and life lessons from Shakespeare's plays; however, these are the treasures that I found.

I hope you find them valuable and intriguing. Each chapter of the book discusses a particular subject and includes relevant text from the plays. I think you will be amazed, as I was, to see how meaningful Shakespeare's words are to us.

ACTION—THE FRUIT OF SPIRITUALITY

Positive spirituality inspires and motivates us toward doing good deeds. Living a spiritual life leads to action and productivity. Spiritual pursuits build a foundation upon which one can reach his or her full potential using abilities, intuition and creative intelligence aimed at laudable goals. The spiritually mature characters of Shakespeare's plays do not spend their lives in repose or continual reflection. They make good things happen and respond to situations with creativity and purpose.

The spiritually energized person seeks opportunities to apply his or her creativity and talent. Even prayer, meditation and imagination require involvement and focus, and these activities prepare a person to take the best actions in any situation.

The unspiritual person is concerned with self, pleasure and security. When the time for action comes, the risk or challenge can appear too threatening to these concerns. Fear, hesitancy and selfishness win the day.

Shakespeare teaches in *Julius Caesar* that there is a time to act quickly and boldly to gain one's dreams:

> There is a tide in the affairs of men,
> Which, taken at the flood, leads on to fortune;
> Omitted, all the voyage of their life
> Is bound in shallows and in miseries.

> On such a full sea are we now afloat;
> And we must take the current when it serves,
> Or lose our ventures. (Act IV, scene iii)

The timid, lazy or fearful soul can easily waste his or her life and not contribute anything of lasting quality. In *The Tempest*, Shakespeare describes such people who lag behind the go-getters:

> Ebbing men, indeed,
> Most often do so near the bottom run
> By their own fear or sloth. (Act II, scene i)

To recognize opportunities and take timely actions, one must develop spiritual insights and awareness coupled with energy and enthusiasm. Often, before we can gain the objects of our goals, life requires a leap of faith, necessitating spiritual values and vision.

Shakespeare recognizes that good intentions must produce actions before any good is created or experienced. In *The Merchant of Venice*, he indicates the uniqueness of people who fulfill their good intentions—people who walk their talk:

> If to do were as easy as to know what were good
> To do, chapels had been churches and poor men's
> cottages princes' palaces. It is a good divine that
> follows his own instructions: I can easier teach
> twenty what were good to be done, than be one of the
> twenty to follow mine own teaching. (Act I, scene ii)

Despite knowing what to do, we do not always do it. Sometimes we would do well to halter our imaginative planning and let our actions catch up to our existing good intentions.

In *King John*, the king is pouting like a sad child and failing to take the initiative regarding urgent matters of the realm. Philip Faulconbridge encourages the King to stand up and behave like a king in force and majesty. His words instruct us during our times of ennui:

> But wherefore do you droop? why look you sad?
> Be great in act, as you have been in thought;
> Let not the world see fear and sad distrust
> Govern the motion of a kingly eye:
> Be stirring as the time; be fire with fire;
> Threaten the threatener, and outface the brow
> Of bragging horror: so shall inferior eyes,
> That borrow their behaviors from the great,
> Grow great by your example, and put on
> The dauntless spirit of resolution.
> Away, and glister like the god of war,
> When he intendeth to become the field:
> Show boldness and aspiring confidence. (Act V, scene i)

All of us are God's creatures created to live boldly and confidently. Shakespeare's words lend themselves to goal setting and persevering through the great challenges in life. When we become resolute in our actions and stand with our heads held high, we can hear the response from Shakespeare, "This becomes the great." (*Henry the Fifth*--Act III, scene v)

ANGELS EVERYWHERE

Shakespeare may never have seen an angel; however, in his plays, he demonstrates a keen awareness of their existence and purpose. To Shakespeare, there exists an unseen spiritual world directed purposefully by a knowing hand.

Through several of his characters, he describes angels' tasks and physical attributes. These angels have a God-given charge to help people and are empowered for good. Shakespeare's characters' thoughts and visions of angels serve to lift their spirits or increase their courage. Shakespeare's descriptions of angels probably differ little from your own ideas about angels.

In *Romeo and Juliet,* Romeo presents an image of a beautiful messenger from heaven when he uses romantic language comparing Juliet to an angel:

> She speaks:
> O, speak again, bright angel! for thou art
> As glorious to this night, being o'er my head
> As is a winged messenger of heaven
> Unto the white-upturned wondering eyes
> Of mortals that fall back to gaze on him
> When he bestrides the lazy-pacing clouds
> And sails upon the bosom of the air. (Act II, scene i)

Who of us would not like to hear ourselves compared to such a creature by our lover? In this brief description,

Shakespeare describes a beautiful, immortal messenger flying to bring good news. This is a comforting thought to anyone believing such an angel is nearby.

I think Shakespeare would counsel us to believe in our guardian angel and to communicate with him during leisure and emergencies.

When all else fails, ask your guardian angel for help as Prince Hamlet does in *Hamlet* when confronted by the unsettling ghost of his dead father. He shouts, "Angels and ministers of grace defend us!" (Act I, scene iv) Believing in the protection of angels, he proceeds to overcome his fear and speak to the ghost.

In *Othello*, Gratiano gasps at the death of his niece Desdemona at the hands of her husband Othello. He grieves for her and is glad her father is not alive to witness her death, because he would be so distraught that he would offend his guardian angel:

> This sight would make him do a desperate turn,
> Yea, curse his better angel from his side,
> And fall to reprobance. (Act V, scene ii)

Shakespeare writes of a guardian angel that only a fool or an incensed man would ever make the mistake of offending.

By describing angels as "ministers of grace" in *Hamlet,* Shakespeare indicates a belief that angels are agents of goodness and favor. Grace is God's favor given freely to people. Angels do good things for us. Sometimes their good deeds are done in response to prayers, while at other times they act according to God's initiative.

In *King Henry the Fifth,* the Archbishop of Canterbury decrees a prayer over the King that angels will keep him safe:

SHAKESPEARE ON SPIRITUALITY

> God and his angels guard your sacred throne,
> And make you long become it! (Act I, scene iv)

This prayer shows a belief system that includes the concept of angels and God working together to answer a person's prayer in accordance to a heavenly purpose.

Shakespeare's view of angels shows them playing a positive role at a person's death. For those who have lived a virtuous and godly life, angels lead them to heaven.

When Queen Katherine loses the favor of the King in *King Henry the Eighth* and dreads her imminent death, an angelic troop visits her during her sleep to assuage her fear and leaves her hopeful and peaceful. She addresses her servant Griffith who, although present when she awakes, does not see the angels:

> Saw you not, even now, a blessed troop
> Invite me to a banquet; whose bright faces
> Cast thousand beams upon me, like the sun?
> They promised me eternal happiness;
> And brought me garlands, Griffith, which I feel
> I am not worthy yet to wear: I shall, assuredly. (Act IV, scene ii)

The inspiring creatures cause Queen Katherine to resent the world and long for the promised eternal banquet of happiness and joy. Experiencing a heavenly vision like this might make any of us run toward death and embrace eternity.

In *Hamlet*, Horatio prays that welcoming angels would accompany Prince Hamlet in death:

> Now cracks a noble heart. Good night, sweet prince,
> And flights of angels sing thee to thy rest! (Act V, scene ii)

Shakespeare assures us that singing, shining, ministering angels accompany us through life and in death.

In the above lines spoken at Prince Hamlet's death, Horatio practices what the prince had previously taught him:

> There are more things in heaven and earth, Horatio,
> Than are dreamt of in your philosophy. (Act I, scene v)

According to Shakespeare, angels are present and waiting to serve us. The next time you are tempted to worry or fear, remember your angels and take courage, or if you are in the midst of trying to win someone's heart, it never hurts to compare him or her to an angel.

APPEARANCES CAN BE DECEIVING

How do we judge people? Whose attention do we desire and whom do we try to impress? What do we consider most important about ourselves: appearance or spiritual maturity? Shakespeare counsels us to beware of those who proffer outward beauty that disguises inner selfishness and unseemly motives. The cliché "do not judge a book by its cover" summarizes Shakespeare's example for sizing up people and for conducting relationships.

Shakespeare places a premium value on loyalty and trust. Some of his characters prodigiously place their trust on unworthy men or women who display a good "show" of loyalty or who mesmerize with beauty and wit. We learn from the plays how to study people and how to guard our hearts and purses from con men and deceiving beauties. In *Much Ado About Nothing*, Claudio warns that not even friendship is secure against the charms of outward beauty:

> Friendship is constant in all other things
> Save in the office and affairs of love:
> Therefore all hearts in love use their own tongues;
> Let every eye negotiate for itself,
> And trust no agent; for beauty is a witch,
> Against whose charms faith melteth into blood. (Act II, scene i)

A person must build his or her faith in unseen spiritual substance to protect against being deceived by what appeals to the senses. One must learn not to be fooled by appearances—both beautiful and ugly. Sometimes we must overlook beauty to see inner corruption, and sometimes we must overlook outward dullness to see virtue within. Antonio, in *Twelfth Night,* advises on appearances:

> In nature there's no blemish but the mind;
> None can be call'd deform'd but the unkind:
> Virtue is beauty, but the beauteous evil
> Are empty trunks o'erflourish'd by the devil. (Act III, scene iv)

Valuing virtue more highly than outward beauty conflicts with our culture, but Shakespeare encourages us to strive against the tide of popular opinion, and that is living by faith.

Bassanio, in *The Merchant of Venice*, makes a life-changing decision based on outward appearances. He wants to marry the lovely heiress Portia, but her father, in addition to bequeathing her a fortune, leaves a daunting challenge to her many suitors. They must open one of three small treasure chests to find the picture of Portia. If they choose the wrong chest, the punishment is life as a bachelor. There are three chests: gold, silver and dull-leaden. We meet two suitors who choose the gold and silver chests because of their beauty; they are sent packing.

Shakespeare presents Bassanio as a man of pure heart with constant motives. He surveys the chests and shares his wisdom concerning beauty and appearances:

> So may the outward shows be least themselves:
> The world is still deceived with ornament.
> In law, what plea so tainted and corrupt,
> But, being seasoned with a gracious voice,
> Obscures the show of evil? In religion,
> What damned error, but some sober brow
> Will bless it and approve it with a text,
> Hiding the grossness with fair ornament?
> There is no vice so simple but assumes
> Some mark of virtue on his outward parts:
> How many cowards, whose hearts are all as false
> As stairs of sand, wear yet upon their chins
> The beards of Hercules and frowning Mars;
> Who, inward search'd, have livers white as milk;
> And these assume but valour's excrement
> To render them redoubted! ...
> Thus ornament is but the guiled shore
> To a most dangerous sea. (Act III, scene ii)

Based on the above wisdom, Bassanio chooses the dull-leaden chest that indeed holds the picture of beautiful Portia inside, and he and Portia marry. His words speak about the efforts we may make to amend our appearance while neglecting our soul and spirit.

The bachelor Prince Pericles makes a similarly wise choice in *Pericles* when he meets the lovely daughter of Antiochus. Antiochus is King of Antioch, and Pericles has come to Antioch to decide whether to marry his daughter; however, Pericles discerns that Antiochus and his daughter have been engaged in an incestuous relationship since the death of the queen. The court of Antioch presents a stately king and pretty princess, and it is corrupted by a pervading evil. Pericles rebuffs the morally corrupt princess as he holds her by the hand:

> Fair glass of light, I loved you, and could still,
> Were not this glorious casket stored with ill:
> But I must tell you, now my thoughts revolt;
> For he's no man on whom perfections wait
> That, knowing sin within, will touch the gate. (Act I, scene i)

Even though he knows the evil activities of the princess, Pericles is still tempted by her beauty. He resists the temptation of deceptive beauty and departs while leaving a warning to beware of evil enshrouded in beauty.

With enough work, a person can glaze over his or her own character shortcomings with contrived appearances and actions. Shakespeare tells us that even "the devil hath power to assume a pleasing shape." (*Hamlet*--Act II, scene ii) To Polonius, in *Hamlet,* man's ability to cover faults makes even the most upright man somewhat suspect of deception. He tells his thoughts to his friend Claudius, who is guilty of his own deception:

> 'Tis too much proved--that with devotion's visage
> And pious action we do sugar o'er
> The devil himself. (Act III, scene i)

King Claudius' reaction ratifies Polonius' words. He has been hiding behind a mask of virtue after murdering his brother, the king. These words seem to strike at his sugar-covered, dark heart; he responds quietly aside:

> O, 'tis too true!
> How smart a lash that speech doth give my conscience!

> The harlot's cheek, beautied with plastering art,
> Is not more ugly to the thing that helps it
> Than is my deed to my most painted word:
> O heavy burden! (Act III, scene i)

King Claudius covers his evil deeds with a crown and all the accouterments of the throne, but he cannot hide his darkness. With enough time in Shakespeare's plays, the light shines through the outward make-up of deceptive characters to expose inner ugliness. The spirit of a person counts for everything; appearances offer temporary cover only.

To demonstrate how a man as evil as perhaps the "devil himself" can adroitly masquerade as a loyal servant and friend, Shakespeare offers Iago, Othello's right-hand man in *Othello*. Iago, seeming the honest friend, is hell-bent on destroying Othello and gaining status for himself. He openly shares his wicked philosophy of deception with his useful companion Roderigo:

> I follow him to serve my turn upon him:
> We cannot all be masters, nor all masters
> Cannot be truly follow'd. You shall mark
> Many a duteous and knee-crooking knave,
> That, doting on his own obsequious bondage,
> Wears out his time, much like his master's ass,
> For naught but provender, and when he's old, cashier'd:
> Whip me such honest knaves. Others there are
> Who, trimm'd in forms and visages of duty,
> Keep yet their hearts attending on themselves,
> And, throwing but shows of service on their lords,
> Do well thrive by them and when they have lined their coats

> Do themselves homage: these fellows have some soul;
> And such a one do I profess myself. For, sir,
> It is as sure as you are Roderigo,
> Were I the Moor, I would not be Iago:
> In following him, I follow but myself;
> Heaven is my judge, not I for love and duty,
> But seeming so, for my peculiar end. (Act I, scene i)

If Shakespeare takes his characters seriously at all, and I believe he does, then he earnestly believes that such men as these evil people exist around us. By presenting characters like Iago and Claudius, Shakespeare warns us to be on guard.

If by chance, you are such a schemer as Iago, you can learn the craft from him. As noted in references to Iago by those he is deceiving, he does it well. Cassio, another target of Iago, grants him approval as the most kind and honest man in the city, and Othello seems willing to place Iago in charge of his very soul:

> This fellow's of exceeding honesty,
> And knows all qualities, with a learned spirit,
> Of human dealings. (Act III, scene iii)

Yet, Iago possesses complete dishonesty and evil intentions in his relations with Othello and Cassio. Their trust in him leads to Othello's mad jealousy that incites him to murder his wife and to take his own life. Cassio survives with an injury. Iago is finally found out for what he truly is and is killed, but due to his skillful deception, he has succeeded in ruining several lives.

Moral and ethical people may wonder how a person can be one thing but pretend to be something else. How can the false man wear such a true face? Shakespeare shows men and women in his plays putting on favorable appearances that hide evil because of their jealousy, greed, selfish ambition and anger. These evil desires subdue the characters' consciences allowing unconscionable behavior.

Both Lady Macbeth and Macbeth in *Macbeth* also demonstrate the process by which loyal and seemingly good people turn to evil. The Macbeths are compelled by greed and selfish ambition; these attributes and their deceptive cunning cause the downfall of their king and ultimately themselves. Their act of murdering the king in order to allow Macbeth to become king requires teamwork. Macbeth does not quickly take to playing the faithful host prior to killing his houseguest, King Duncan. Lady Macbeth instructs him in the ways of falsehood lest his appearance betray his guilt:

> Your face, my thane, is as a book where men
> May read strange matters. To beguile the time,
> Look like the time; bear welcome in your eye,
> Your hand, your tongue: look like the innocent flower,
> But be the serpent under't. (Act I, scene v)

This chide of Lady Macbeth can go into the instruction manual for backstabbing. These evil characters offer glimpses of the vices existing in real people. The average person may have difficulty imagining the hypocrisy and wickedness of a Lady Macbeth or an Iago; however, for the false person, the task of deception is all too comfortable.

Malcolm, the son of the murdered king in *Macbeth*, says to his brother regarding the difficulty of identifying those guilty of the murder:

> To show an unfelt sorrow is an office
> Which the false man does easy. (Act II, scene iii)

Shakespeare advises us to know those we trust and to study them thoroughly before letting down our guard and jeopardizing our well-being. Look through appearances and into the spirit and heart of a man or woman.

Prior to his death in *Macbeth*, King Duncan, the first victim of the Macbeths, explains the vulnerability that leads to his misplaced trust in people and ultimately his death. He speaks of his betrayal by the previous Thane of Cawdor, a man once trusted by the king:

> There's no art
> To find the mind's construction in the face:
> He was a gentleman on whom I built an absolute
>   trust. (Act I, scene iv)

One must wonder whether Shakespeare would advise placing an absolute trust in anyone besides God. By taking into account his insights into the weaknesses of people, I think he would advise having only a guarded trust in any person that we do not know inside and out.

APPROVAL FROM PEOPLE COMES AND GOES

Even the most spiritually grounded people are often swayed from their course by an interest in gaining approval from others. A spiritual direction in life usually leads to considerable solitude, prayer, study, and humility to gain a God-centered vision and purpose. In conflict with this direction, people possess a seemingly innate desire to gain high opinions and approval from people important to them in some way. If we give into this temptation, we make decisions in life based on the opinions of others—real or imagined. In his plays, Shakespeare demonstrates the slipperiness of the approval of other people, showing that it is nothing on which to base self-esteem, confidence or decisions.

In *Julius Caesar*, we see two characters, Flavius and Marullus, rebuking the cheering crowds welcoming Caesar to Rome after his defeat of Pompey in battle. They rebuke the commoners because their homage now made to Caesar was in the recent past made as earnestly to Pompey:

> You blocks, you stones, you worse than senseless things!
> O you hard hearts, you cruel men of Rome,
> Knew you not Pompey? Many a time and oft
> Have you climb'd up to walls and battlements,
> To towers and windows, yea, to chimney-tops,

> Your infants in your arms, and there have sat
> The livelong day, with patient expectation,
> To see great Pompey pass the streets of Rome:
> And when you saw his chariot but appear,
> Have you not made an universal shout,
> That Tiber trembled underneath her banks,
> To hear the replication of your sounds
> Made in her concave shores?
> And do you now put on your best attire?
> And do you now cull out a holiday?
> And do you now strew flowers in his way
> That comes in triumph over Pompey's blood? Be gone!
> Run to your houses, fall upon your knees,
> Pray to the gods to intermit the plague
> That needs must light on this ingratitude. (Act I, scene i)

Whether it is a crowd cheering or one person patting your back, it comes and goes. The wise person bases his or her life on something of more substance and permanency than the positive or negative opinions of other people. As is the case in *Julius Caesar*, those who applaud us today may scorn us tomorrow.

Celebrities such as actors, singers, and athletes usually have flocks of people crooning and fawning over them—as long as they are successful. Make a bad movie, a song that doesn't sell, or fail in the big game and the mood changes to boos, disdain or, even worse, to apathy and abandonment by the fans. This is also true in our private lives. When fortune smiles on us, people seek our company or association; fair-weather friends stick by the people picking up the tab, but they are nowhere to be found when the tab comes for them to pay the price of friendship with help or support.

The Greek warrior Achilles describes in *Troilus and Cressida* this ebb and flow in relationships based on ulterior or selfish motives:

> 'Tis certain, greatness, once fall'n out with fortune,
> Must fall out with men too: what the declined is
> He shall as soon read in the eyes of others
> As feel in his own fall; for men, like butterflies,
> Show not their mealy wings but to the summer,
> And not a man, for being simply man,
> Hath any honour, but honour for those honours
> That are without him, as place, riches, favour,
> Prizes of accident as oft as merit:
> Which when they fall, as being slippery standers,
> The love that lean'd on them as slippery too,
> Do one pluck down another and together
> Die in the fall. (Act III, scene iii)

One of the blessings in living a spiritual life and seeking God is finding the fellowship of like-minded people. Bonds between people based on spiritual truths and love do not break under the strains of trials; in fact, it is during trials and in the tough times that such bonds perform great service. A true friend sticks beside us when we are in or out of favor with fortune.

Regarding the affections of people, Shakespeare gives brief but sound advice through the Duke in *Measure for Measure* that addresses the desire to impress others and gain their approval:

> I love the people,
> But do not like to stage me to their eyes:
> Though it do well, I do not relish well
> Their loud applause and Aves vehement;
> Nor do I think the man of safe discretion
> That does affect it. (Act I, scene i)

The Duke mistrusts the person who caters to the applause of others. To make decisions based on gaining people's approval instead of on principled values prevents one from being true to his or her convictions and vision. Shakespeare would encourage us to find out who we are, to find our true calling and to live according to it rather than what others might think or say about us.

ATTITUDE, ATTITUDE, ATTITUDE

Shakespeare recognizes the power of the mind in determining happiness and the course of one's life. He teaches that we can transform negative thinking to positive life-changing thoughts.

The belief that we control our thoughts and can change our attitudes emphasizes the superiority of the spirit in the human trinity of spirit, soul and body. A person's spirit has power to change thoughts and emotions. The spirit determines perceptions of events in life; and thus, the spirit determines, ultimately, our actions. A positively charged and hopeful spirit inspires confident and optimistic thoughts and emotions; conversely, a spirit that lacks power and motivation generates thoughts of failure and emotions of despair, fear and worry. Our spirit is the core of who we are—our heart.

How we see the world affects our place and role in it. Shakespeare produces an excellent example of this in *King Richard the Second*. King Richard banishes Henry Bolinbroke from England for ten years. Henry despairs at the sentence and complains to his father, John of Gaunt. John of Gaunt attempts to assuage his son's grief by arguing for a change of perception about the banishment. He wants his son to consider it an opportunity to see the world and mature through experiences abroad. He suggests an attitude adjustment for his son:

> All places that the eye of heaven visits
> Are to a wise man ports and happy havens.
> Teach thy necessity to reason thus;
> There is no virtue like necessity.
> Think not the king did banish thee,
> But thou the king. Woe doth the heavier sit,
> Where it perceives it is but faintly borne.
> Go, say I sent thee forth to purchase honour
> And not the king exiled thee; or suppose
> Devouring pestilence hangs in our air
> And thou art flying to a fresher clime:
> Look, what thy soul holds dear, imagine it
> To lie that way thou go'st, not whence thou comest:
> Suppose the singing birds musicians,
> The grass whereon thou tread'st the presence strew'd,
> The flowers fair ladies, and thy steps no more
> Than a delightful measure or a dance;
> For gnarling sorrow hath less power to bite
> The man that mocks at it and sets it light. (Act I, scene iii)

According to Shakespeare's wisdom, we can completely change how we experience life by changing our perception, thoughts and emotions concerning the events of our lives. The power to control our thoughts and emotions lies within each of us. Like Bolingbroke, counseled to see the negative punishment in a positive light, we are counseled by Shakespeare to reframe situations and events that could otherwise affect us negatively.

Prince Hamlet shares this view in a conversation with Rosencrantz in *Hamlet*. He declares that a thing can be considered positively or negatively depending on a person's perception of it, "for there is nothing either good or bad, but thinking makes it so." He emphasizes this truth further by saying, "I could be bound in a nut shell and count myself a king of infinite space." (Act II, scene ii) This truth is life changing, because we can direct our thoughts through spiritual discipline.

I imagine a present-day Shakespeare performing as a motivational speaker energizing audiences with proclamations like that of King Henry V inspiring his army at the Battle of Agincourt in *King Henry the Fifth:* "All things are ready, if our minds be so." Of course, he would demand the audience shout in unison a reply similar to that of Westmoreland: "Perish the man whose mind is backward now!" (Act IV, scene iii)

CHARACTER MATTERS

The way a person relates to others flows from his or her character. Whether a person treats others the way he or she wants to be treated in return or in a selfish manipulative manner indicates good or bad character. Character is not natural or automatic in people. Good or bad character is taught, nurtured and developed.

Character flaws are weaknesses in a person's moral fortitude; we all have them to some degree. They are not necessarily permanent and can be overcome by engaging in spiritual activities to live more wholesomely. Shakespeare recognizes that character flaws left untreated can grow and blossom until they actually define a person.

In *The Second Part of King Henry the Fourth*, Warwick predicts the growth of Northumberland's character flaw that is his inclination to betray people. He therefore warns King Henry IV not to trust him:

> There is a history in all men's lives,
> Figuring the nature of the times deceased;
> The which observed, a man may prophesy,
> With a near aim, of the main chance of things
> As yet not come to life, which in their seeds
> And weak beginnings lie intreasured.
> Such things become the hatch and brood of time;
> And by the necessary form of this,

> King Richard might create a perfect guess
> That great Northumberland, then false to him,
> Would of that seed grow to a greater falseness;
> Which should not find a ground to root upon,
> Unless on you. (Act III, scene i)

We usually overlook minor character flaws in friends, family or associates, and especially in "yours truly," but we may want to address those flaws lest they grow and become a cancer on the entire person. We should make a habit of examining ourselves for character flaws grown hairy over the years.

Our character can be so refined and honest that even those who oppose us or disagree with us would speak well of us. If people recognize that someone has a good heart and is genuine in dealings with others, they give that person the benefit of the doubt when questions arise. Gaining trust from others and keeping it requires good character. In *Julius Caesar*, Marc Antony testifies to the good character of his fallen enemy Brutus:

> This was the noblest Roman of them all:
> All the conspirators, save only he,
> Did that they did in envy of great Caesar;
> He only, in a general honest thought,
> And common good to all, made one of them.
> His life was gentle; and the elements
> So mixt in him, that Nature might stand up
> And say to all the world, 'This was a man!' (Act V, scene v)

When a person consistently seeks to do good and not evil, it is apparent in the perception of his character by those who know him or her. Good or bad character cannot be hidden from others for long; it will speak for itself.

In *Hamlet*, Hamlet esteems men who possess character stronger than the temptations that could undermine their devotion:

> Give me that man
> That is not passion's slave, and I will wear him
> In my heart's core, ay, in my heart of heart. (Act III, scene ii)

This statement implies that men who put integrity above selfish gain or pleasure are rare jewels and, when found, should be treasured. What Hamlet seeks is a man of good character.

The opposite of the above quote is true of men whose character is not based on principle. Such were the three Englishmen who were set to betray King Henry V as he prepared to make war on France. In *King Henry the Fifth*, Shakespeare describes them as "hollow bosoms" tempted to betrayal by the French offer of "treacherous crowns." If our hearts are not filled with truth and virtue, our integrity has a price, and our character can be hijacked by greed, lust, ambition, covetousness or fear. These men had been friends and advisors to the king, but they sell themselves for a price.

A CHEERFUL HEART

Shakespeare's plays reflect his insight into the connections between a person's mind, emotions and body. He expresses in *The Taming of the Shrew* that cheerfulness is good for a person's complete health and that the opposite is also true: prolonged sadness leads to poor health. In the play's introduction, a messenger announces the arrival of actors to perform an uplifting entertaining play (a play within the play) for a character who has been in a state of sadness:

> Your honour's players, hearing your amendment,
> Are come to play a pleasant comedy;
> For so your doctors hold it very meet,
> Seeing too much sadness hath congeal'd your blood,
> And melancholy is the nurse of frenzy:
> Therefore they thought it good you hear a play
> And frame your mind to mirth and merriment,
> Which bars a thousand harms and lengthens life.
>   (Intro, scene ii)

The spiritual person is a humorous person—not taking anything too seriously and ready to laugh heartily at the slightest entertainment. Possessing a constant joy, we remain energized, and our bodies and minds can dispel fatigue, sickness and distress.

Shakespeare was a playwright, an entertainer, who wrote

several plays for sheer comedy. He expected audiences at his comedies to sit back and laugh. Ultimately, his plays exist to entertain and to inspire audiences to return to the theater for the next play. The success of his plays indicates not only their entertainment value but also their underlying power to move the audience's emotions in a spiritual manner that produces a feeling of being alive, leading to an uplifted and cheerful heart.

CONTENTMENT ABOVE ALL THINGS

The consumerism of our culture is at odds with contentment. The purpose of the plethora of advertisements that barrage us daily is to convince us to want what we do not have. A person may possess all he or she needs for a happy life, but if he or she lives in perpetual want of something else, the result can be misery. In Shakespeare's plays, the discontented poor and lowly envy the rich nobles, and restless kings covet the free carelessness of the servants; in both cases, the coveted prize is contentment.

In *King Henry the Fifth*, King Henry decries the useless ceremony and accouterments of the crown. He laments that the throne does not, in all of its majesty, provide him peace, rest, cheerfulness or power to heal the sick and poor. With all of his honor and majesty, he envies the sleeping commoner and his imagined dreams.

While walking among his sleeping subjects, King Henry V ponders the value of peace and rest compared to the value of the crown:

> What infinite heart's-ease must kings neglect,
> That private men enjoy!
> And what have kings, that privates have not too,
> Save ceremony, --save general ceremony?
> And what art thou, thou idol ceremony?...
> Canst thou, when thou command'st the beggar's knee,

Command the health of it? No, thou proud dream,
That play'st so subtly with a king's repose;
I am a king that find thee, and I know
'Tis not the balm, the sceptre and the ball,
The sword, the mace, the crown imperial,
The intertissued robe of gold and pearl,
The farced title running 'fore the king,
The throne he sits on, nor the tide of pomp
That beats upon the high shore of this world,
No, not all these, thrice-gorgeous ceremony,
Not all these, laid in bed majestical,
Can sleep so soundly as the wretched slave,
Who with a body fill'd and vacant mind
Gets him to rest, cramm'd with distressful bread;
Never sees horrid night, the child of hell,
But, like a lackey, from the rise to set
Sweats in the eye of Phoebus and all night
Sleeps in Elysium; next day after dawn,
Doth rise and help Hyperion to his horse,
And follows so the ever-running year,
With profitable labour, to his grave:
And, but for ceremony, such a wretch,
Winding up days with toil and nights with sleep,
Had the fore-hand and vantage of a king.
The slave, a member of the country's peace,
Enjoys it; but in gross brain little wots
What watch the king keeps to maintain the peace,
Whose hours the peasant best advantages. (Act IV, scene i)

Nothing in the kingdom of England could afford the King a night of peaceful rest. We do not have the worries of ruling a kingdom, but sometimes in ruling our lives, we submit ourselves to excessive work or commitments that profit us much less than they cost us in peace and contentment.

Shakespeare does not counsel us to give up our duties, plans or careers just so we can have a good night's sleep. I think he promotes good judgment, so we expend our energies in fulfilling our calling and producing lasting gain instead of striving after what we really do not need.

King Henry VI is willing to give up the crown and his riches to live a pastoral life without the concerns of the country. In *The Third Part of King Henry the Sixth*, King Henry VI speaks of contentment in relation to the crown:

> My crown is in my heart, not on my head;
> Not decked with diamonds and Indian stones,
> Nor to be seen: my crown is called content:
> A crown it is that seldom kings enjoy. (Act III, scene i)

King Henry VI is right on target when he values his spiritual crown from heaven more than the crown of England that will pass away. Shakespeare, however, does not lead us to believe that seeking contentment justifies abdicating the duty we have to do good works. King Henry VI behaves apathetically toward the throne and its intrinsic power for good or evil, and it eventually falls into the hands of the evil Richard III who strives to obtain it. While valuing his spirituality, the king still needs to perform his duties.

We may make all sorts of changes in our lives to gain contentment and find that we are still wanting. Contentment comes through faith, trust and satisfaction in the blessings of God. Nothing can satisfy all of our physical and worldly desires. They are continually tantalized, but God satisfies the desires of the heart of a person who seeks him more than anything else in life, whether he or she is king or pauper.

Contentment comes from within, and it pays a higher salary than any amount of income. In *The Merchant of Venice*, the wise character Portia counsels, "He is well paid that is well satisfied." (Act IV, scene i) Spirituality does not incorporate escapism. Through spiritual pursuits, we find and fulfill our true calling and destiny in life and find joy in the process.

DEATH—HEAVEN OR HELL

Shakespeare's view of the spiritual life extends beyond this earth and this body. His plays examine heaven and hell and the mystery of life after death. His presentations of the positive and negative expectations of eternity give us plenty of reasons to examine our ways on earth and how they might affect our eternity.

If King Hamlet, in *Hamlet*, could return from the grave and live life on earth again, he might do a few things differently. His deeds cause him to end up in a state of purgatory, as his soul is purged of evil. He does manage to come back from this tormenting state of limbo to warn his son Prince Hamlet and to urge him unto vengeance, and we see a hint of his afterlife, which seems to be a temporary hell. As he appears to his son, he describes his current state and how he ended up there:

> My hour is almost come,
> When I to sulphurous and tormenting flames
> Must render up myself….
> I am thy father's spirit,
> Doom'd for a certain term to walk the night,
> And for the day confined to fast in fires,
> Till the foul crimes done in my days of nature
> Are burnt and purged away. But that I am forbid
> To tell the secrets of my prison-house,
> I could a tale unfold whose lightest word

> Would harrow up thy soul, freeze thy young blood,
> Make thy two eyes, like stars, start from their spheres,
> Thy knotted and combined locks to part
> And each particular hair to stand on end,
> Like quills upon the fretful porpentine:
> But this eternal blazon must not be
> To ears of flesh and blood...
> Thus was I, sleeping, by a brother's hand
> Of life, of crown, of queen, at once dispatcht:
> Cut off even in the blossoms of my sin,
> Unhousell'd, disappointed, unanel'd,
> No reckoning made, but sent to my account
> With all my imperfections on my head:
> O, horrible! O, horrible! most horrible! (Act I, scene v)

According to his confession made to Prince Hamlet, the King's season in hell is a result of his brother's murdering him while he was in a sinful state and unprepared for death. The King is destined for heaven but only after a time of serious and painful purging. This type of spiritual belief in purgatory undoubtedly would contribute to Prince Hamlet's hesitancy to take vengeance against his murdering uncle or to harm himself when he contemplates suicide later in the play.

Prince Hamlet hesitates in exacting revenge, because he also fears he might have been betrayed by a deceptive ghost from hell, and maybe his uncle is innocent. As he despairs, he contemplates taking his own life. From this contemplation, we have Shakespeare's famous soliloquy by Hamlet as he discusses the mysteries of what consequences his considered actions might bring:

SHAKESPEARE ON SPIRITUALITY

To be, or not to be,--that is the question:--
Whether 'tis nobler in the mind to suffer
The slings and arrows of outrageous fortune,
Or to take arms against a sea of troubles,
And by opposing end them?--To die,--to sleep,--
No more; and by a sleep to say we end
The heart-ache and the thousand natural shocks
That flesh is heir to, 'tis a consummation
Devoutly to be wisht. To die,--to sleep,--
To sleep! perchance to dream: ay, there's the rub;
For in that sleep of death what dreams may come
When we have shuffled off this mortal coil,
Must give us pause: there's the respect
That makes calamity of so long life;
For who would bear the whips and scorns of time,
The oppressor's wrong, the proud man's contumely,
The pangs of despised love, the law's delay,
The insolence of office and the spurns
That patient merit of the unworthy takes,
When he himself might his quietus make
With a bare bodkin? who would fardels bear,
To grunt and sweat under a weary life,
But that the dread of something after death,
The undiscover'd country from whose bourn
No traveller returns,--puzzles the will
And makes us rather bear those ills we have
Than fly to others that we know not of?
Thus conscience does make cowards of us all;
And thus the native hue of resolution
Is sicklied o'er with the pale cast of thought,
And enterprises of great pith and moment
With this regard their currents turn awry,
And lose the name of action. (Act III, scene I)

Although any person has power to escape this world by taking his or her own life, few take this option because of the unknown reality of life after death and because of humans' instinctual drive toward self-preservation. People also refrain from other actions, even those of "great pith and moment," because their outcomes are unknown and because the downside outweighs the opportunity for reward. Prince Hamlet, at this point, lacks clarity in the course of action he should take. He wavers between vengeance and escaping life altogether. At the forefront of his thoughts, the vast unchartered sea of death intimidates him.

Prince Hamlet has not been helped by his mother, the Queen, who would like him to accept the death of his father and get over it. She wishes to deny the severity of the loss and continue living a comfortable life. She advises her son:

> Good Hamlet, cast thy nighted colour off,
> And let thine eye look like a friend on Denmark.
> Do not for ever with thy vailed lids
> Seek for thy noble father in the dust:
> Thou know'st 'tis common,--all that lives must die,
> Passing through nature to eternity. (Act I, scene ii)

The Queen eventually faces the reality of her shameful involvement with Claudius, the murderer of his brother and her husband. Shakespeare demonstrates in *Hamlet* that all actions have consequences in this life and in the next, and we should live according to how we want to spend eternity rather than living only for our pleasure. As Shakespeare writes, this is a temporary home, and eternity is forever. How we live our lives has enormous consequences for eternity.

Shakespeare offers glimpses of the pangs or peace of

departing souls as they exit this world for a better or worse place. In *The Second Part of King Henry the Sixth*, we see the departing soul of the hypocritical, conspiring, greedy Cardinal Beaufort. As King Henry VI prays for mercy on his soul, we see the result of the Cardinal's evil life. The following dialogue at his deathbed indicates a fearful introduction to death and a reckoning for his guilt. His involvement in murder and conspiracy haunt him on his deathbed:

> KING HENRY VI
> How fares my lord? speak, Beaufort, to
> thy sovereign.
>
> CARDINAL BEAUFORT
> If thou be'st death, I'll give thee England's treasure,
> Enough to purchase such another island,
> So thou wilt let me live, and feel no pain.
>
> KING HENRY VI
> Ah, what a sign it is of evil life,
> Where death's approach is seen so terrible!
>
> WARWICK
> Beaufort, it is thy sovereign speaks to thee.
>
> CARDINAL
> Bring me unto my trial when you will.
> Died he not in his bed? Whe'r should he die?
> Can I make men live, whether they will or no?
> O, torture me no more! I will confess.
> Alive again? then show me where he is:
> I'll give a thousand pound to look upon him.

He hath no eyes, the dust hath blinded them.
Comb down his hair; look, look! it stands upright,
Like lime-twigs set to catch my winged soul.
Give me some drink; and bid the apothecary
Bring the strong poison that I bought of him.

KING HENRY VI
O thou eternal Mover of the heavens.
Look with a gentle eye upon this wretch!
O, beat away the busy-meddling fiend
That lays strong siege unto this wretch's soul.
And from his bosom purge this black despair!

WARWICK
See, how the pangs of death do make him grin!

SALISBURY
Disturb him not; let him pass peaceably.

KING HENRY VI
Peace to his soul, if God's good pleasure be!
Lord cardinal, if thou think'st on heaven's bliss,
Hold up thy hand, make signal of thy hope.
He dies, and makes no sign. O God, forgive him!

WARWICK
So bad a death argues a monstrous life.

KING HENRY VI
Forbear to judge, for we are sinners all.
Close up his eyes and draw the curtain close;
And let us all to meditation. (Act III, scene iii)

Cardinal Beaufort, a religious leader who had abandoned his spiritual duty and conspired in murder for political gain, experiences the consequences of his unrepented guilt. His example inspires King Henry VI to encourage all of the onlookers to contemplate their own spiritual state and readiness for death. Nothing in life for which the Cardinal has compromised his integrity to possess or experience is worth the price he pays in torment. Sir William Catesby in *King Richard the Third* summarizes, "'Tis a vile thing to die, my gracious lord, when men are unprepared and look not for it." (Act III, scene ii)

If the above description of the Cardinal's death does not inspire you to take inventory of your spiritual state, maybe Othello's last words in *Othello* will lead you to actions to avoid his eternal resting place. During his mad jealousy, he kills his virtuous wife Desdemona. As he looks at her dead body, his guilt and shame portend his banishment to hell that he describes:

> Where should Othello go?
> Now, how dost thou look now? O ill-starr'd wench!
> Pale as thy smock! when we shall meet at compt,
> This look of thine will hurl my soul from heaven,
> And fiends will snatch at it. Cold, cold, my girl!
> Even like thy chastity.
> O cursed slave! Whip me, ye devils,
> From the possession of this heavenly sight!
> Blow me about in winds! roast me in sulphur!
> Wash me in steep-down gulfs of liquid fire!
> O Desdemona! Desdemona! dead! (Act V, scene ii)

Shakespeare emphasizes the evil power of greed, jealousy and selfish ambition to drive men and women to do evil acts that lead their souls to the care of "fiends" and "devils." He demonstrates that no actions are worth taking when the eternal consequence is so costly.

Shakespeare also provides glimpses of happy souls moving onward to heaven. Prior to his murder in *King Richard the Second,* King Richard II offers his vision of a better place awaiting his soul:

> Mount, mount, my soul! thy seat is up on high;
> Whilst my gross flesh sinks downward, here to die.
>   (Act V, scene v)

The body stays below to return to the earth, but according to Shakespeare, the spirit and soul continue to live. The spirit of Juliet in *Romeo and Juliet* ascends to heaven leaving the Friar and Romeo to grieve over her body. The Friar tries to comfort Romeo with the thought that she is better off in heaven than she was on earth:

> Heaven and yourself
> Had part in this fair maid; now heaven hath all,
> And all the better is it for the maid:
> Your part in her you could not keep from death,
> But heaven keeps his part in eternal life. (Act IV,
>   scene v)

Shakespeare shares the same comfort that is often expressed by and to mourners to help them accept a loved one's death: the person has left the trials of this world to enter into the peace and happiness of heaven. It is easier for mourners to accept a loved one's death when they can believe that the person continues to live in a better place. For some people, it might be the case, and for others, it might not be true.

On the Agincourt battlefield in *King Henry the Fifth,* Shakespeare alludes to the comfort gained in heaven. Exeter describes the death of the Earl of Suffolk and the Duke of York. This scene demonstrates the hopefulness of a dying person possessing faith in heaven as his or her eternal home:

> Suffolk first died: and York, all haggled over,
> Comes to him, where in gore he lay insteep'd,
> And takes him by the beard; kisses the gashes
> That bloodily did yawn upon his face;
> And cries aloud 'Tarry, dear cousin Suffolk!
> My soul shall thine keep company to heaven;
> Tarry, sweet soul, for mine, then fly abreast,
> As in this glorious and well-foughten field
> We kept together in our chivalry!' (Act IV, scene vi)

In this scene, we see the hope of being with loved ones and friends in heaven. If heaven exists, then as Shakespeare suggests, we would indeed be with family and friends forever in happiness; however, we cannot presume entrance into heaven for ourselves or others. All of us must examine our lives and seek the truth regarding heaven and hell and to where we would go if death comes today.

Life offers no guarantees regarding the number of our years. Shakespeare counsels us to prepare today to face death, because its coming is definite and not according to our schedule. In *Pericles,* Pericles ponders the fragile existence of people:

> Whereby I see that Time's the king of men,
> For he's their parent, and he is their grave,
> And gives them what he will, not what they crave.
> (Act II, scene iii)

Let us hope and plan to live long prosperous lives but also prepare our souls and spirits for life's end, as if it is due today.

DEMONS AND WITCHES

In his plays, Shakespeare presents good and evil, light and darkness, God and Satan, and angels and demons. Some characters pray to God for blessings, and conversely, some characters seek benefits and guidance from the forces of darkness. These dark forces present themselves in hideous forms. They possess some knowledge of the future, and through their persuasion, they negatively influence events in the plays.

Shakespeare does not use the term "selling your soul to the devil," but he certainly describes the process of people throwing themselves to the devil's care to gain brief glory and power on earth. In Shakespeare's plays, I don't think there exists a more explicit illustration of evil's influence on a character's life than in *Macbeth*. Macbeth and his wife let messengers of demons from hell guide their steps and inspire their actions. Because of the prescient words of three witches, the Macbeths' lives are ruined, multiple people are killed, and a nation is torn.

In the beginning of the play, when returning from a battle, Macbeth and Banquo are met by three witches, later called the "strange sisters" by Macbeth. At this time, Macbeth bears the title "thane of Glamis." The witches call him not only "thane of Glamis" but also "thane of Cawdor," and they predict he shall be called king in the future. The witches practice sorcery, and although their predictions might come true, the final outcome is destruction and cannot be otherwise for the Macbeths, since they bind themselves to demons and witches.

Following this pleasant prediction to Macbeth by the witches, Banquo entreats them for a prediction concerning him. They eagerly grant his request and state that although he will not be king his offspring shall be kings. The witches hail Banquo and Macbeth with flattery due to their foreseen honors.

Soon after the statements are made, the witches disappear in a cloud of smoke, and riders come to declare that Macbeth has pleased the king and has been named the new thane of Cawdor. This fulfills one of the witches' predictions giving credibility to all they have said of Macbeth and Banquo.

Shakespeare demonstrates a useful tool of the forces of darkness in deceiving people. He shows how evil messengers lure people into evil activities by appealing to a person's desire for knowledge and by appealing to pride, greed, selfish ambition, lust, envy, etc. Through Banquo's reaction to the announcement that the king has named Macbeth thane of Cawdor as the witches predicted, Shakespeare shares a truth about evil's tactics:

> What, can the devil speak true?
> ...But 'tis strange:
> And oftentimes, to win us to our harm,
> The instruments of darkness tell us truths,
> Win us with honest trifles, to betray's
> In deepest consequence. (Act I, scene iii)

Banquo's caution is well-founded. The prediction teases him with the thought that his offspring will be kings, but he beholds from where the prediction has come and to where it could lead if he were to take it to heart.

Macbeth, on the other hand, immediately begins to see

himself as king and to plot in his mind how it can happen. The sudden prediction and fulfillment of being named thane of Cawdor ignites in him ambition and lust for power that were previously suppressed by contentment to serve the king. Now he contemplates rising to that very office regardless of the evil acts that must bring it to pass. This one message from the witches transforms him into a person void of contentment and peace. He has thus been inspired to become king, even if the task ruins his life. He speaks aside to himself of such thoughts:

> (Aside) Two truths are told,
> As happy prologues to the swelling act
> Of the imperial theme...
> This supernatural soliciting
> Cannot be ill, cannot be good: if ill,
> Why hath it given me earnest of success,
> Commencing in a truth? I am thane of Cawdor:
> If good, why do I yield to that suggestion
> Whose horrid image doth unfix my hair
> And make my seated heart knock at my ribs,
> Against the use of nature? Present fears
> Are less than horrible imaginings:
> My thought, whose murder yet is but fantastical,
> Shakes so my single state of man that function
> Is smother'd in surmise, and nothing is
> But what is not. (Act I, scene iii)

Macbeth becomes desperate for power and bound to the evil foretelling of these witches. He overlooks their wickedness, their sources of knowledge, their strange concoctions and lack of genuine care for his well-being. He loses all reason and care of good and evil, because he seeks only to satisfy his ambition. As he gains the fulfillment of their prediction that he will be king, he loses all that is good in his life, including his soul.

In his desperation to rule as king, he seeks the witches again for knowledge. This time he sees and hears from the witches' masters, their demons. Their messages reveal the true essence of their motives: blood, death, war and discord. In Macbeth, they find a willing vessel through whom to work. They leave him mad, enraged and despairing for his life, yet he has dug himself into a pit from which he cannot escape. As he departs from where they have spoken to him, he condemns himself for his foolishness in listening to them, "damned all those that trust them!"

In *Macbeth*, words spoken by the ugliest creatures imaginable have led to the murder and downfall of great men and women. Macbeth even had his minions kill his former friend Banquo in an attempt to void the witches' predictions regarding Banquo's offspring.

Macbeth is not the only play in which Shakespeare presents characters communicating with fallen angels. In *The First Part of King Henry the Fourth*, Owen Glendower boasts of his ability to command evil spirits. He tells Henry Percy (Hotspur),

> I can call spirits from the vasty deep...
> I can teach you, cousin, to command the devil. (Act III, scene i)

On the next day, Henry Percy recounts his night spent in the field with Glendower:

> He held me last night at least nine hours
> In reckoning up the several devil's names

That were his lackeys. (Act III, scene i)

In the plays, nothing good comes to those who invoke such wicked spirits to gain help or knowledge. Glendower and his side are defeated in their civil war by King Henry's armies.

In *The Second Part of King Henry the Sixth*, a conjurer, Roger Bolingbroke, and a witch, Margaret Jourdain, call forth a demon to ask it about the fates of various other characters. They call up a demonic spirit named Asmath. Bolingbroke counsels the witch concerning their deeds of darkness involving the demon:

> Patience, good lady; wizards know their times:
> Deep night, dark night, the silent of the night,
> The time of night when Troy was set on fire;
> The time when screech-owls cry and ban-dogs howl,
> And spirits walk and ghosts break up their graves,
> That time best fits the work we have in hand.
> Madam, sit you and fear not: whom we raise,
> We will make fast within a hallow'd verge. (Act I, scene iv)

When they have received the requested information from the spirit, Bolingbroke commands it to return to "darkness and the burning lake," leaving no mystery regarding its nature. Their sorcery party is crashed by authorities from court, and Bolingbroke and Jourdain are taken into custody for their practice of witchcraft and sorcery.

None of the characters invoking evil spirits by sorcery has any doubts about the evil nature of the spirits they invoke; however, the characters are so greedy for power and control they are willing to consort with messengers of hell rather than trust in providence. Contentment is a virtue unknown to those who are willing to give up everything for worldly glory. Anytime external forces influence our thoughts and dreams, we should first analyze the motives and character of the source and then consider the consequences of buying into the message.

DEPRESSION AND DESPAIR: ENEMIES WITHIN

Depression is living without joy and resembles a slow death more than life. Depression describes a spiritual void, a black hole in the soul. During depression, that place in our hearts that should be filled with hope, joy, light, and peace lies vacant and dark. During depression, the mind possess a bleak vision of the future that causes despair.

A person's experience of depression may last a brief time or can last years. Shakespeare offers insights into the nature of the depressed person. Some of his characters become mired in despair due to their perceptions of life's circumstances.

In *Romeo and Juliet*, Romeo exhibits the type of depression that can follow disappointment due to lost love, failure, or trouble. His father notices Romeo's depression and shares his observations with his nephew Benvolio:

> Many a morning hath he there been seen,
> With tears augmenting the fresh morning dew.
> Adding to clouds more clouds with his deep sighs;
> But all so soon as the all-cheering sun
> Should in the farthest east begin to draw
> The shady curtains from Aurora's bed,
> Away from the light steals home my heavy son,
> And private in his chamber pens himself,
> Shuts up his windows, locks fair daylight out,

> And makes himself an artificial night:
> Black and portentous must this humour prove,
> Unless good counsel may the cause remove. (Act I, scene i)

Romeo's depression seems perhaps vain or melodramatic, since it is based on a girl's rejection of him; however, to the depressed person, reason succumbs to emotion. Shakespeare wisely suggests that "good counsel" can benefit the depressed person.

Romeo's depression also includes an inner sense of foreboding born out of a lack of hope. To him, his future does not appear bright. Although he throws up his course to providence, his attitude appears more guided by despair than trust in God. He explains his dark foreboding feeling,

> …for my mind misgives
> Some consequence yet hanging in the stars
> Shall bitterly begin his fearful date
> With this night's revels and expire the term
> Of a despised life, closed in my breast
> By some vile forfeit of untimely death.
> But He, that hath the steerage of my course,
> Direct my sail! (Act I, scene iv)

Romeo's intuition warns him to practice caution in his actions, but he continues his ill-advised course. Whenever we ignore spiritual messages from God or our own spirit's insight, we become conflicted between soul and spirit, mind and heart. This internal disconnection often initiates depression. A person falling into depression needs to refresh and reenergize himself spiritually instead of following, like Romeo, a reckless and desperate path.

No Shakespearean character may be more conflicted than Prince Hamlet in *Hamlet*. His spirit guides him in one way and his mind and emotions in another. His internal conflict causes depression and despair to such an extent that he longs for death, and he admits that if suicide were not eternally frowned upon it might be his preferred option. His vision lacks hope or optimism, and to him, the world seems haunting and void of pleasure. He bemoans his life, the world and God's decrees, and he wishes he could excuse himself from them all:

> O, that this too too solid flesh would melt,
> Thaw, and resolve itself into a dew!
> Or that the Everlasting had not fixt
> His canon 'gainst self-slaughter! O God! God!
> How weary, stale, flat, and unprofitable,
> Seem to me all the uses of this world!
> Fie on't! ah fie! 'tis an unweeded garden,
> That grows to seed; things rank and gross in nature
> Possess it merely. (Act I, scene ii)

Depression and despair are emotional and spiritual bullies. Their heavy burden causes their victims to look longingly for ways out of their grasp. Severe depression often leads to self destruction. To the depressed person, there seems to be nothing in the world that could bring pleasure or laughter.

Consider Louis, Prince Dauphin of France, in *King John*. His words succinctly describe how a depressed person might view the world:

> There's nothing in this world can make me joy:
> Life is as tedious as a twice-told tale
> Vexing the dull ear of a drowsy man;

> And bitter shame hath spoil'd the sweet world's taste
> That it yields naught but shame and bitterness. (Act III, scene iv)

Depression vexes a person inwardly with shame and bitterness. Venturing out into the world seems threatening and without reward for the depressed person, so isolation and loneliness occur.

In *The Second Part of King Henry the Fourth*, King Henry IV becomes sad as he contemplates his enemies with whom he had once been friends. He surmises that if one could read the open book of one's fate and fortune in this life, one would choose to forfeit said life rather than face its ills:

> O, if this were seen,
> The happiest youth, viewing his progress through,
> What perils past, what crosses to ensue,
> Would shut the book, and sit him down and die. (Act III, scene i)

Despair often results from contemplation of the vanity of one's life. King Henry IV realizes his crown was purchased at the cost of friendships, peace, rest and contentment. All of these things that were lost cannot be regained, and despair overshadows any hope of enjoying what was gained at so high of a price. Shakespeare points to the "crosses" we face, referencing the cross of Christ, a destined suffering that must be endured.

What might be helpful to the depressed person is a friend lending a listening ear or extending a comforting hand. I think Shakespeare might counsel the depressed person to seek joy again in friendly relationships or in positive spiritual activities like prayer, scriptures, songs or just sitting in God's presence letting his light and love lift one's spirit. At the top of Shakespeare's list of cures for a lingering depression would probably be watching a funny play or movie.

DIVINE RIGHTS OF ALL

Many of Shakespeare's plays involve the royalty of kingdoms. Men and women strive to claim thrones and power by rightful lineage or by usurpation or war. In his plays, Shakespeare discusses a belief (especially popular among reigning kings) that attributes election of kings to providence. According to this belief, a king reigns because God has anointed him to reign. Widely held, this belief would protect the king from rivals. Surely, no man would presume to oppose God's will by opposing or dethroning God's anointed.

In *King Richard the Second,* King Richard II claims the argument of the divine rights of kings in his attempt to gird up his support against the rebellious Henry Bolingbroke:

> Not all the water in the rough rude sea
> Can wash the balm off from an anointed king;
> The breath of worldly men cannot depose
> The deputy elected by the Lord:
> For every man that Bolingbroke hath prest
> To lift shrewd steel against our golden crown,
> God for his Richard hath in heavenly pay
> A glorious angel: then, if angels fight,
> Weak men must fall, for heaven still guards the right.
> (Act III, scene ii)

Later in the play, the Bishop of Carlisle, a supporter of

King Richard, confirms his own belief in the divine rights of kings as he rebukes Henry Bolingbroke and others who would usurp King Richard's crown:

> And shall the figure of God's majesty,
> His captain, steward, deputy elect,
> Anointed, crowned, planted many years,
> Be judged by subject and inferior breath,
> And he himself not present? O, forfend it, God,
> That in a Christian climate souls refined
> Should show so heinous, black, obscene a deed!
> I speak to subjects, and a subject speaks,
> Stirr'd up by God, thus boldly for his king. (Act IV, scene i)

The Bishop of Carisle claims actually to speak for God on behalf of the king and emphasizes the correlation between anointed by God and crowned.

Henry Bolingbroke seeks the throne from King Richard partly because the king has confiscated his family's estate following the death of his father, John of Gaunt. John of Gaunt, however, might counsel his son against taking up arms against the king. In *King Richard the Second*, John of Gaunt refuses to revenge a brother's death because of his respect for the position of king, whom he refers to as God's minister:

> God's is the quarrel; for God's substitute,
> His deputy anointed in His sight,
> Hath caused his death: the which if wrongfully,
> Let heaven revenge; for I may never lift
> An angry arm against His minister. (Act I, scene ii)

Perhaps this is the attitude we should have regarding all people when we are tempted to take vengeance or speak harmfully against someone.

The idea of the divine rights of kings does not stay the hands of all usurpers or murderers of kings in Shakespeare's plays. In *King Richard the Second,* Henry Bolingbroke eventually takes Richard II's crown and a supporter of Bolingbroke, on his own initiative, takes the life of Richard II. However, the transgression of harming the king stands out blacker than other crimes due to the belief that he or she is in authority according to God's will. The exception occurs when the king lives a horribly evil life like King Richard III or Claudius in *Hamlet.* If one gains the throne by ignoring the divine right of the previous king, he or she certainly cannot expect to invoke the belief for his or her reign.

Shakespeare adeptly summarizes the question of divine rights of kings in the play *The Winter's Tale.* Camillo, a servant of Leontes, King of Silicia, is ordered by Leontes to murder Polixenes, the King of Bohemia. Camillo knows Polixenes is innocent of the accusations levied by Leontes, and he refuses to commit murder. He verbalizes his reaction to the order:

> But, for me,
> What case stand I in? I must be the poisoner
> Of good Polixenes; and my ground to do't
> Is the obedience to a master; one
> Who, in rebellion with himself, will have
> All that are his so too. To do this deed,
> Promotion follows. If I could find example
> Of thousands that had struck anointed kings
> And flourisht after, I'ld not do't; but since
> Nor brass nor stone nor parchment bears not one,

> Let villany itself forswear't. I must
> Forsake the court: to do't, or no, is certain
> To me a break-neck. Happy star, reign now! (Act I, scene ii)

Camillo refuses to act against a king based on the absence in history of men who have flourished after killing a king. He perceives that the act would condemn him to a miserable consequence, so he flees Leontes' court rather than fulfill his evil command.

In *Macbeth,* Macduff describes the murder of King Duncan as an act mightily opposed to spiritual virtues. He compares the king to the Lord's temple:

> Most sacrilegious murder hath broke ope
> The Lord's anointed temple, and stole thence
> The life o' th' building! (Act II, scene iii)

Shakespeare emphasizes the heinous nature of the murder or betrayal of kings; however, the same spiritual laws apply to the murder or betrayal of any person.

God's concern for a king is no more significant than his concern for you or me. The belief in the divine rights of kings is a belief that God possesses a purpose and design for the king's life. The same is true for each of us. We each have a divine right to pursue God's will for our lives and to strive to fulfill our fullest potential as positive and creative human beings. Any person who opposes our honest pursuit of this vision opposes God's plan and attempts to steal the life in God's temple.

We have the responsibility to live like honorable kings

seeking to fulfill God's good purpose and not our own selfish gains. Similarly, we would do well to interact with others in light of the idea that they also have divine rights as humans.

DRUNKENNESS LEADS TO STUMBLING

People seeking positive experiences in life or a respite from negativity often over indulge in alcohol as a means to lose themselves in revelry or solace. Alcohol lubricates inhibitions and devours self-consciousness. Some individuals drink alone to numb emotional pain. Drinking too much alcohol becomes an obstacle to positive spirituality and to living a fulfilling life. Alcohol appeals to our desire to live life to the hilt; however, it leads those who succumb to its appeal to a darkened spiritual void.

In Shakespeare's play *Othello*, the devilish Iago uses alcohol as a weapon against Cassio, Othello's lieutenant. Iago who is plotting to set the friends Cassio and Othello against one another by trickery knows Cassio's weakness toward drunkenness.

He prods Cassio into drinking too much alcohol; Cassio protests prior to acquiescing to Iago's demands. He describes his poor reactions to alcohol,

> Not to-night, good Iago: I have very poor and unhappy brains for drinking: I could well wish courtesy would invent some other custom of entertainment….
>
> …I have drunk but one cup to-night, and that was craftily qualified too, and, behold, what innovation it makes here: I am unfortunate in the infirmity,

> and dare not task my weakness with any more. (Act II, scene iii)

Cassio demonstrates his awareness of his weakness for alcohol and for the dangers associated with becoming drunk. Shakespeare shows that even in the 17th Century peer pressure leads to drunkenness and stupid behaviors.

Cassio gives in to Iago's pressure to drink, becomes drunk and is set up by Iago's friend Roderigo to become enraged. He ends up wounding Montano, an official of the city and predecessor of Othello, with a sword. Othello shows up at the scene and finds Cassio drunk on duty and guilty of stabbing a prominent citizen. Othello strips Cassio of his commission of Lieutenant.

Cassio laments his actions and his drinking to Iago, and he rightly labels the drink that has led to his stupidity:

> O thou invisible
> spirit of wine, if thou hast no name to be known by, let us call thee devil! (Act II, scene iii)

Wine may not be the devil itself, but it has certainly been used by the devil throughout history to tempt men and women and lead them to debauchery and awful consequences. Cassio's actions agree with Shakespeare's description of alcoholic drinks in *As You Like It* as "hot and rebellious liquors." Still, people everywhere turn compulsively to such drinks again and again in attempts to gain a spiritual high or to numb pains.

Cassio summarizes the events related to his drunkenness and anger:

> I remember a mass of things, but nothing distinctly;
> a quarrel, but nothing wherefore. O God, that men
> should put an enemy in their mouths to steal away
> their brains! that we should, with joy, pleasance
> revel and applause, transform ourselves into beasts!
> ...It hath pleased the devil drunkenness to give place
> to the devil wrath; one unperfectness shows me
> another, to make me frankly despise myself. (Act II,
> scene iii)

Shakespeare shows the typical outcome of drunkenness: loss of reason, regret and spite for one's self. The appeal of alcohol is the promise of joy, peace, laughter, fellowship and self-confidence among other positive experiences, yet the true delivery of alcohol and drunkenness is, in the end, none of these but is a loss of true identity and divine purpose.

EVIL NATURE OF HUMANS

Shakespeare does not exhibit a naïve view of human nature. He illustrates the best of humanity in some of his noble and loving characters, and he presents characters of selfishness, greed, cruelty and utter evil to balance the scale of his reflection of humanity's behavior. Shakespeare's insights into the nature of evil not only create believable characters for his plays but also enlighten his audiences regarding what lurks in the shadows of the hearts and minds of people. Unfortunately, we learn that in some people the shadows consume any spark of light and leave the person without any governing virtue.

Characters that kill children and women, rape and torture, steal and betray are presented not as fantastic or surreal but as true-to-reality, wicked people. We are made to believe that the evil in Shakespeare's most unseemly characters does not exaggerate or embellish what might exist in our neighbors, civic leaders, co-workers or family members. In some of his characters, the evil grows from a minor character flaw; in others, evil consumes them completely.

In *Titus Andronicus,* Shakespeare presents shockingly cruel characters. Two sons of the Queen of Goth living in Rome kill the brother of the Roman Emperor while he and Lavinia, the daughter of Titus Andronicus, a Roman General, are riding horses in a forest. They proceed to rape Lavinia and then cut out her tongue and cut off her hands and leave her in the forest. The two brothers then frame Lavinia's own two brothers for the crime, and they are put to death prior to their exoneration. This represents the normal behavior of the Goths according to Shakespeare. It also represents the worst of humanity.

Another character in the play, Aaron, the Queen of Goth's lover, verbalizes the thoughts and attitudes of people who do unthinkable evil to others. As he is about to be executed for his heinous crimes, instead of offering remorse for his complicity in the evil deeds described above, he avows his wickedness, and he regrets that he has not committed more similarly evil deeds:

> Ay, that I had not done a thousand more.
> Even now I curse the day--and yet, I think,
> Few come within the compass of my curse,--
> Wherein I did not some notorious ill,
> As kill a man, or else devise his death,
> Ravish a maid, or plot the way to do it,
> Accuse some innocent and forswear myself,
> Set deadly enmity between two friends,
> Make poor men's cattle break their necks;
> Set fire on barns and hay-stacks in the night,
> And bid the owners quench them with their tears.
> Oft have I digg'd up dead men from their graves,
> And set them upright at their dear friends' doors,
> Even when their sorrows almost were forgot;
> And on their skins, as on the bark of trees,
> Have with my knife carved in Roman letters,
> 'Let not your sorrow die, though I am dead.'
> Tut, I have done a thousand dreadful things
> As willingly as one would kill a fly,
> And nothing grieves me heartily indeed
> But that I cannot do ten thousand more. (Act V, scene i)

Aaron is a character who truly revels in harming others. The evil that Aaron and the Goths perform in this play plagues the community like a virus. Every wicked deed affects the victim, the victim's family and friends, and the community. Because of the act of violence against Lavinia and her companion, all of the Goths involved are killed, two of Titus' sons are killed, Lavinia and Titus are killed, and the emperor Saturninus is killed.

In *Titus Andronicus*, Shakespeare pointedly teaches that evil must be expunged urgently from individuals and the community before it blossoms and inflicts damage and pain upon all.

If left unfettered, conscienceless people proudly continue to do evil. Aaron describes his will to do evil:

> I am no baby, I, that with base prayers
> I should repent the evils I have done:
> Ten thousand worse than ever yet I did
> Would I perform, if I might have my will; (Act V,
>   scene iii)

We hope not to encounter such a malicious person as Aaron; however, if we do, we cannot overestimate his or her potential for doing harm.

Prince Hamlet describes a character flaw or weakness that can exist in a person and can grow to corrupt his or her entire life. He describes this fault as possibly being present at birth—a natural thing perverted, or maybe Shakespeare describes what today we would call a "genetic predisposition" toward evil behavior. In either case, Shakespeare does not proffer an excuse for evil behavior in his explanation of it:

> So, oft it chances in particular men,
> That for some vicious mole of nature in them,
> As, in their birth--wherein they are not guilty,
> Since nature cannot choose his origin--
> By the o'ergrowth of some complexion,
> Oft breaking down the pales and forts of reason,
> Or by some habit that too much o'er-leavens
> The form of plausive manners, that these men,
> Carrying, I say, the stamp of one defect,
> Being nature's livery, or fortune's star,--
> Their virtues else--be they as pure as grace,
> As infinite as man may undergo--
> Shall in the general censure take corruption
> From that particular fault: the dram of eale
> Doth all the noble substance of a doubt
> To his own scandal. (Act I, scene iv)

Shakespeare describes a flaw that can be detrimental to even great leaders and people of seemingly flawless virtue. It may be a weakness such as lust toward the opposite sex, greed, lying, addiction, or a similar vulnerability that undermines all of the other positive character attributes of a person.

An example of this type of singular perversion that Shakespeare describes takes place in the play *Pericles*. The King of Antioch, Antiochus, is a widower with a daughter. He pursues an attraction to his daughter and has a long-standing incestuous relationship with her. Shakespeare describes the sin:

> This king unto him took a fere,
> Who died and left a female heir,
> So buxom, blithe, and full of face,

> As heaven had lent her all his grace;
> With whom the father liking took,
> And her to incest did provoke:
> Bad child; worse father! to entice his own
> To evil should be done by none:
> But custom what they did begin
> Was with long use account no sin. (Act I, prologue)

The king's lust corrupts his life, family and his kingdom, and it all grows from a seed of lust that he may have suppressed while his wife lived. However, once acted upon, the lust consumes his life and actions. In time, their evil relationship even becomes accepted as normal.

Other characters in Shakespeare's plays use evil means in attempts to satisfy their selfish ambitions for power. Selfish ambition arises as the most common character flaw leading to evil actions in the plays. Such actions are not committed for the sake of the experience but for sake of the goal the actions achieve.

In *The Second Part of King Henry the Fourth*, Northumberland, who leads the rebellion against King Henry IV, encourages his band of leaders and soldiers to throw off all moral restraints in their efforts to win control of the kingdom:

> Now let not Nature's hand
> Keep the wild flood confined! let order die!
> And let this world no longer be a stage
> To feed contention in a lingering act;
> But let one spirit of the first-born Cain
> Reign in all bosoms, that, each heart being set
> On bloody courses, the rude scene may end,
> And darkness be the burier of the dead! (Act I, scene i)

The selfishly ambitious person justifies all actions based on the end in mind and forsakes virtues to gain the object of desire. As Northumberland does, he or she may also rally others to the selfish cause, manipulating them with persuasive, emotional words.

The character of King Richard III personifies selfish ambition and evil nature. He rejects all moral restraints in order to gain the crown of England. He commits himself to the vilest acts for his gain and explains his motivation in *The Third Part of King Henry the Sixth* before taking the first step:

> Then, since this earth affords no joy to me,
> But to command, to check, to o'erbear such
> As are of better person than myself,
> I'll make my heaven to dream upon the crown,
> And, whiles I live, to account this world but hell,
> Until my mis-shaped trunk that bears this head
> Be round impaled with a glorious crown.
> And yet I know not how to get the crown,
> For many lives stand between me and home:
> And I--like one lost in a thorny wood,
> That rents the thorns and is rent with the thorns,
> Seeking a way and straying from the way;
> Not knowing how to find the open air,
> But toiling desperately to find it out--
> Torment myself to catch the English crown:
> And from that torment I will free myself,
> Or hew my way out with a bloody axe.
> Why, I can smile, and murder whiles I smile,
> And cry 'Content' to that which grieves my heart,
> And wet my cheeks with artificial tears,
> And frame my face to all occasions.

> I'll drown more sailors than the mermaid shall;
> I'll slay more gazers than the basilisk;
> I'll play the orator as well as Nestor,
> Deceive more slily than Ulysses could,
> And, like a Sinon, take another Troy.
> I can add colours to the chameleon,
> Change shapes with Proteus for advantages,
> And set the murderous Machiavel to school.
> Can I do this, and cannot get a crown?
> Tut, were it farther off, I'll pluck it down. (Act III, scene ii)

Like anyone living unreservedly for self, Richard disavows himself from all affectations toward other people. He would not allow any reason for sympathy or affection toward a person blocking his way to the crown. Later in the same play, he banishes love from himself. Even though he has two brothers and other family, he declares,

> I have no brother, I am like no brother;
> And this word 'love,' which graybeards call divine,
> Be resident in men like one another
> And not in me: I am myself alone. (Act V, scene vi)

Power creates a deceptive draw upon men and women causing them to forsake all good things in life to have it. Richard proceeds to cause the death of countless men, women and children—including his own brothers and nephews.

Power is a fleeting mist that creates a mirage of satisfaction to the seeker, but when gained, it dissipates into sand of anxiety, fear, resentment and paranoia. In Shakespeare's plays, the selfishly ambitious person hungers after power like a savage dog eyeing red meat. With caution, humility and contentment, we must guard ourselves against the negative draw and effect that power can have.

Contentment would have saved Macbeth and his wife from their ill-fated ends in *Macbeth*. Both Macbeths submit themselves to their evil passions. Macbeth stumbles over his conscience at times but is prodded onward by his wife, who has consigned her soul to wicked spirits and cruelty. She recognizes the possibility of Macbeth becoming king and foresees the murder of King Duncan that must occur. As she submits herself to the lust of ambition, she rejects virtue and womanhood and asks dark spirits to come aid her in evil works:

> The raven himself is hoarse
> That croaks the fatal entrance of Duncan
> Under my battlements. Come, you spirits
> That tend on mortal thoughts, unsex me here,
> And fill me from the crown to the toe top-full
> Of direst cruelty! make thick my blood;
> Stop up th' access and passage to remorse,
> That no compunctious visitings of nature
> Shake my fell purpose, nor keep peace between
> The effect and it! Come to my woman's breasts,
> And take my milk for gall, you murd'ring ministers,
> Wherever in your sightless substances
> You wait on nature's mischief! Come, thick night,
> And pall thee in the dunnest smoke of hell,
> That my keen knife see not the wound it makes,
> Nor heaven peep through the blanket of the dark,
> To cry 'Hold, hold!' (Act I, scene v)

Lady Macbeth prays to evil spirits to remove from her path any obstacle of conscience or weak nature, and she asks them for security from heavenly angels who might try to prevent the murder of the king. Her lust for more power causes her to knowingly clash with heaven.

She is not the only woman in Shakespeare's plays whose ambition causes contempt for her womanhood. In *The Second Part of King Henry the Sixth*, the Duchess of Gloucester, who is married to the uncle of King Henry VI, is eager for her husband to usurp the crown from his nephew. Her ambition is greater than his. He rebukes her for suggesting that he should take the throne:

> O Nell, sweet Nell, If thou dost love thy lord,
> Banish the canker of ambitious thoughts! (Act I,
>   scene ii)

Shakespeare demonstrates that ambitious thought is indeed a canker that can grow to overtake virtue and moral character. The Duchess, like Lady Macbeth, seeks to usurp her husband's role. She privately responds to her husband's rebuke of her ambition,

> While Gloucester bears this base and humble mind.
> Were I a man, a duke, and next of blood,
> I would remove these tedious stumbling-blocks
> And smooth my way upon their headless necks;
> And, being a woman, I will not be slack
> To play my part in Fortune's pageant. (Act I, scene ii)

In carrying out her mischievous plans, she consorts with a witch and sorcerer, and they are put to death for treason. Selfish ambition for power leads to numerous deaths in Shakespeare's plays.

In *The First Part of King Henry the Fourth,* Prince Henry kills the rebellious Henry Percy on the battlefield. While looking over the body, he comments on the vanity of misguided ambition:

> For worms, brave Percy: fare thee well, great heart!
> Ill-weaved ambition, how much art thou shrunk!
> When that this body did contain a spirit,
> A kingdom for it was too small a bound;
> But now two paces of the vilest earth
> Is room enough: (Act V, scene iv)

Shakespeare reminds us that we all return to dust, and what we gain in this world is temporary and often not worth the sacrifice we must pay to have it. Prince Henry esteems Henry Percy as a noble and brave man but recognizes his fatal flaw.

Through Macbeth's laments and torment, Shakespeare shows the value of spiritual assets as opposed to temporal gains such as position, worldly treasure and power over others. Macbeth gains the kingdom but loses what would bring him joy and satisfaction. As he makes his last stand against his enemies seeking to overthrow him, he yells for his servant Seyton and proclaims his regrets for following his evil-inspired ambition:

> I am sick at heart,
> When I behold--Seyton, I say!--This push
> Will chair me ever, or dis-seat me now.
> I have lived long enough: my way of life

> Is fall'n into the sear, the yellow leaf;
> And that which should accompany old age,
> As honour, love, obedience, troops of friends,
> I must not look to have; but, in their stead,
> Curses, not loud but deep, mouth-honour, breath,
> Which the poor heart would fain deny, and dare not.
> (Act V, scene iii)

The selfishly ambitious person gives up what cannot be lost to gain what cannot be kept. As soon as the Macbeths gain the throne, they become consumed with keeping it, and they still lose everything.

Each day we have choices to serve God and others or to serve our negative passions. Shakespeare shows us the vanity in following the objects that feign to satisfy our worldly desires. We would be wise and, through it all, happier if we seek what the Macbeths forsake: honor, love, obedience and friends.

FEAR LESS

If there is a negative quality that disrupts our lives and prevents our maturing spiritually more than any other thing, it must be fear. Fear is like paralyzing venom. Shakespeare says, "Of all base passions fear is most accurst." (*The First Part of King Henry the Sixth*--Act V, scene ii) It comes to cause worry about tomorrow—what may come and what may not come. Fear prohibits the pursuit of dreams and the fulfillment of desires.

Shakespeare connects fear with the doubts that challenge our creative ideas and desires. In *Measure for Measure*, Lucio encourages Isabella not to be ruled by her doubts or fears:

> Our doubts are traitors
> And make us lose the good we oft might win
> By fearing to attempt. (Act I, scene iv)

Shakespeare is fully aware of the fears and doubts that come to mind seconds after we have a remarkable idea of some good deed we can accomplish. These doubts betray us and hinder our creativity and actions. In *Macbeth*, Shakespeare again relates fear as a traitor to us:

> When our actions do not,
> Our fears do make us traitors. (Act IV, scene ii)

Fear betrays dreams, promises, commitments and capabilities. It leads to negative emotions, thoughts and actions causing sadness and foreboding; whereas, hope leads to joyful expectation and confidence.

In *The Merchant of Venice*, Solanio, a friend to the merchant Antonio, describes how imagining negative outcomes leads to fear and sadness:

> And every object that might make me fear
> Misfortune to my ventures, out of doubt
> Would make me sad. (Act I, scene i)

Much of our fear deals with fear of loss—loss of possessions, people, status, health, careers, etc. Loss often causes sadness and grief. When we imagine future losses, we begin to fear the loss and grieve as though it has happened already, and usually the loss never happens as we imagine. So often, fear results from our imagination rather than reality.

Shakespeare even describes the sense of fear that sometimes envelopes people without apparent causes. This fear spreads by rumor, panic, or vague feelings of being afraid. In *King John*, Shakespeare describes the contagion of fear:

> As I travell'd hither through the land,
> I find the people strangely fantasied;
> Possest with rumours, full of idle dreams,
> Not knowing what they fear, but full of fear: (Act IV, scene ii)

This is a lesson to guard against baseless fears. Fear behaves like a slinking thief that creeps and crawls through any opening in our armor to come and disturb our peace and prevent the initiation and fulfillment of good deeds.

SHAKESPEARE ON SPIRITUALITY

In *King Henry the Fifth,* Shakespeare offers advice for combating rising fear, "the greater therefore should our courage be." (Act IV, scene i) Courage, after all, is only necessary in the face of things that reasonably make us fear. When after reason and logic determine that a fear is based on truth, Shakespeare still counsels us to have courage instead of fear:

> Why, courage, then! What cannot be avoided
> 'Twere childish weakness to lament or fear.
> (*The Third Part of King Henry VI*--Act V, scene iv)

What we must face, we can face with courage. The spiritual person does not fear the many setbacks that threaten people every day. Even death is not feared when faced with hope and faith. We live joyfully by hoping for the good and not fearing the worst. In *Measure for Measure*, when he is facing the death penalty, Claudio, who is innocent, takes courage and proclaims, "I've hope to live, and am prepared to die." (Act III, scene i)

The most spiritually mature person cannot avoid the trials and losses of life; however, we can grow beyond living in fear to live lives based on truth, hope and faith. Shakespeare says, "true nobility is exempt from fear." (*The Second Part of King Henry VI*--Act IV, scene i)

FRIENDSHIPS MAKE LIFE WORTH LIVING

No character in Shakespeare's plays enjoys happiness without possessing at least one close friend. Though a character possesses the throne, wealth, status or beauty, without a trustful confidant, he or she lacks satisfaction and contentment. Friendship produces benefits that cannot be experienced in any other way. In his plays, we see friends who share possessions, reputation, counsel, encouragement, comfort, forgiveness and merriment. Friendship stands out in the plays as one of the spiritual riches that should be sought and enjoyed throughout life.

In *The Two Gentlemen of Verona*, a strong friendship between the two main male characters is esteemed, tested, betrayed and restored. The play begins with Proteus and Valentine saying their "good-byes" as Valentine leaves Verona for Milan. They tender much affection and loyalty toward each other, displaying their bond of friendship. Later, due to his sexual attraction to Valentine's sweetheart Silvia, Proteus betrays Valentine and seeks to seduce Silvia. When Valentine apprehends Proteus in the act of practically forcing himself upon her, Valentine is offended and broken-hearted as he learns that Proteus has betrayed him.

We see in this dialogue the value of friendship to Shakespeare, as well as the shame of betrayal and the honor of repentance and forgiveness. Valentine confronts Proteus who promptly requests forgiveness from Valentine:

VALENTINE
Thou common friend, that's without faith or love,
For such is a friend now; treacherous man!
Thou hast beguiled my hopes; naught but mine eye
Could have persuaded me: now I dare not say
I have one friend alive; thou wouldst disprove me.
Who should be trusted, when one's right hand
Is perjured to the bosom? Proteus,
I am sorry I must never trust thee more,
But count the world a stranger for thy sake.
The private wound is deepest: O time most accurst,
'Mongst all foes that a friend should be the worst!

PROTEUS
My shame and guilt confounds me.
Forgive me, Valentine: if hearty sorrow
Be a sufficient ransom for offence,
I tender 't here; I do as truly suffer
As e'er I did commit.

VALENTINE
Then I am paid;
And once again I do receive thee honest.
Who by repentance is not satisfied
Is nor of heaven nor earth, for these are pleased.
By penitence th' Eternal wrath's appeased:
And, that my love may appear plain and free,
All that was mine in Silvia I give thee. (Act V, scene iv)

Shakespeare presents an accurate portrayal of friendship rather than an ideal relationship void of ups and downs.

Valentine and Proteus experience a conflict of a sort that could very well end a friendship, but both recognize the value of their bond. It is worth it to Proteus to ask for forgiveness and worth it to Valentine to grant forgiveness. In Shakespeare's plays and in life, intimate, worthwhile relationships experience conflict and, therefore, require apologies and forgiveness.

To enjoy honest friendships, friends must practice forgiveness and have realistic expectations for their relationships. Through Cassius in *Julius Caesar*, Shakespeare states an axiom to uphold in friendships. During an argument, Cassius says to his friend and comrade Brutus that "a friend should bear his friend's infirmities." To be a friend, we need to overlook our friends' minor shortcomings and accept them as they are.

Sharing support and counsel are two ubiquitous uses of friends in the plays. Every human needs them both from time to time. We would all be wealthy in friends if we had one friend like the character Timon of Athens. In *Timon of Athens*, Timon explains that one should support his friends in their time of need. If friends do not provide help, they are not friends but useless acquaintances, he explains:

> ...what need we have any
> friends, if we should ne'er have need of 'em? they
> were the most needless creatures living, should we
> ne'er have use for 'em, and would most resemble
> sweet instruments hung up in cases that keep their
> sounds to themselves. (Act I, scene ii)

Timon literally puts his money where his mouth is for his friends who come to him asking for his support. He willingly helps those he perceives as his true friends.

One such person is Ventidius who has landed himself in debtor's prison. He sends his servant to ask Timon for the ransom. In his response, Timon shares his generous thoughts and attitude toward friends:

> TIMON
> Noble Ventidius! Well;
> I am not of that feather to shake off
> My friend when he must need me. I do know him
> A gentleman that well deserves a help:
> Which he shall have: I'll pay the debt,
> and free him.
>
> VENTIDIUS' MESSENGER
> Your lordship ever binds him.
>
> TIMON
> Commend me to him: I will send his ransom;
> And being enfranchised, bid him come to me.
> 'Tis not enough to help the feeble up,
> But to support him after. (Act I, scene i)

Timon behaves generously; unfortunately, he does not receive the same support in return from his friends. When his fortune is spent, none of his friends bails him out or even sympathizes with him; they abandon him.

Shakespeare's lesson is clear: as important as friends are, it is equally important to weigh their trustworthiness prior to investing abundantly in the relationship. Shakespeare confirms the lesson in *Henry the Eighth.* The Duke of Buckingham offers this advice regarding the relation of friends to one's personal fortune:

> This from a dying man receive as certain:
> Where you are liberal of your loves and counsels
> Be sure you be not loose; for those you make friends
> And give your hearts to, when they once perceive
> The least rub in your fortunes, fall away
> Like water from ye, never found again
> But where they mean to sink ye. (Act II, scene i)

This statement summarizes the experience of Timon of Athens. It is a heartbreak of betrayal that leads to his lonely death. We do not need to make the same mistake, because we know to guard our hearts and choose our friends carefully.

Besides gaining support from friends in times of need, we depend on friends for counsel and listening ears. When we need to vent our emotions, confess our mistakes or just get things off our chest, non-judgmental friends are priceless. In *The Winter's Tale*, Leontes, the King of Sicilia, has benefited greatly from his friendship with Camillo. He explains how he has shared the secrets of his heart:

> I have trusted thee, Camillo,
> With all the nearest things to my heart, as well
> My chamber-councils, wherein, priest-like, thou
> Hast cleansed my bosom,--I from thee departed
> Thy penitent reform'd: (Act I, scene ii)

It is wonderful to feel cleansed from burdens, anxieties, guilt and fears. A friend with whom one can share honestly allows us to release the cares of our hearts.

In Leontes' case, he unfortunately loses the benefit of his friendship with Camillo when he falsely accuses him of helping the Queen have an affair with Leontes' childhood friend. There is nothing like jealous rage to ruin a friendship or marriage.

Shakespeare reminds us to be a friend to ourselves as we are to others. In *King Henry the Eighth*, the Duke of Norfolk advises his friend the Duke of Buckingham to use for himself the same wisdom with which he has counseled others:

> Not a man in England
> Can advise me like you: be to yourself
> As you would to your friend. (Act I, scene i)

Whenever you are in a predicament, think how you would advise a friend in that same predicament, and then take your own advice.

After all Shakespeare writes of friendships, we know loyal, loving, wise friends are not a dime a dozen. When we find a good one, we should nurture that relationship, building it and making it stronger:

> Those friends thou hast, and their adoption tried,
> Grapple them to thy soul with hoops of steel; (*Hamlet*
>   Act I, scene iii)

GRIEF: A NECESSARY PART OF LIFE

Most people we meet have experienced a deep, permeating grief. Life is full of loss, and loss produces grief and sorrow. Grief can penetrate the very marrow of our souls. While grief can eventually lead to profound understanding of life and spirituality, it can also overwhelm and mire us in a well of despair and sadness or of anger and resentment. Contemporary grief counselors do not guide people away from grief but rather lead people through a healthy, appropriate grieving process. There were no grief counselors in the 17th century; Shakespeare, however, offers counsel to those who grieve. His words inform us about the healthy way to handle our grief and how we can support grieving friends.

His first lesson concerns the differing opinions of grief held by those suffering the loss versus mere bystanders to the loss. Shakespeare discusses the heaviness of grief to the one suffering and encourages sympathy for him or her. He writes in *Much Ado About Nothing* that "every one can master a grief but he that has it." (Act III, scene ii) Handling grief seems easy and matter-of-fact to the outsider, but when it is upon you, the load is not so easy.

Later in *Much Ado About Nothing,* the character Leonato, Governor of Messina, chides his brother for attempting to assuage his grief before it has run its course for the apparent loss of his daughter Hero:

> Men
> Can counsel and speak comfort to that grief
> Which they themselves not feel; but, tasting it,
> Their counsel turns to passion, which before
> Would give preceptial medicine to rage,
> Fetter strong madness in a silken thread,
> Charm ache with air and agony with words:
> No, no; 'tis all men's office to speak patience
> To those that wring under the load of sorrow,
> But no man's virtue nor sufficiency
> To be so moral when he shall endure
> The like himself. Therefore give me no counsel:
> My griefs cry louder than advertisement. (Act V, scene i)

Shakespeare, through Leonato, discourages us from preventing loved ones from grieving and experiencing sadness for loss. It is common for people to feel uncomfortable around mourners, but mourning with weeping and sadness is a healthy expression of grief that not only needs to be tolerated but encouraged and supported.

Grief can cause people to question God and their spirituality. Anger at God may be one of the first reactions by people who feel the pain of loss.

In *Macbeth*, there is no shortage of death, and no character may feel it more than Macduff. His wife and children are butchered in Scotland by Macbeth's henchman while Macduff pursues help in England. When he hears the news of their deaths, he is bewildered and shocked. Malcom, the son of the murdered King Duncan, encourages him to speak lest his heart break with grief. Then Malcom exhorts him to satisfy his grief in seeking revenge against Macbeth. Macduff counters that he must be allowed to feel the loss of his family before taking action against their murderers:

> I shall do so;
> But I must also feel it as a man:
> I cannot but remember such things were,
> That were most precious to me. Did heaven look on,
> And would not take their part? Sinful Macduff,
> They were all struck for thee! naught that I am,
> Not for their own demerits, but for mine,
> Fell slaughter on their souls. Heaven rest them now!
>   (Act IV, scene iii)

Macduff cannot believe his family is lost to him; he feels anger and wonder at God. He also feels guilty that he was not there to protect them. Malcolm correctly asks Macduff to share his feelings verbally. After speaking from his heart, Macduff proceeds to channel these feelings into delivering vengeance upon Macbeth, so his grief serves him well in victory. Most of us cannot work out our grief by killing our enemy, so we must work through our feelings and try to overcome the loss.

Having friends or family to share loss with us is like having a friend help us move a couch through a narrow door way. Even with two people, the couch is still heavy and awkward to move, but moving a couch by oneself goes slowly and painfully, if at all. Shakespeare looks to friends to help lighten the awkward and heavy load of grief. In *King Lear*, Edgar's grief seems to shrink when he gains the fellowship of King Lear who is also grieving his misfortune. Edgar explains his change of feelings at seeing King Lear grieve,

> When we our betters see bearing our woes,
> We scarcely think our miseries our foes.
> Who alone suffers suffers most i' the mind,
> Leaving free things and happy shows behind:
> But then the mind much sufferance doth o'er skip,
> When grief hath mates, and bearing fellowship.
> How light and portable my pain seems now,
> When that which makes me bend makes the king bow. (Act III, scene vii)

Our own grief is acute and seems unique to us; however, it is lightened by having partners in the episode.

During times of grief, we may feel alone as Constance does in *King John* following the loss of her son. She describes her grief as being too heavy for her or anyone to bear:

> …my grief's so great
> That no supporter but the huge firm earth
> Can hold it up. (Act III, scene i)

Constance also describes her grief as occupying every space vacated by the loss of her son. In such cases, may God bless us with friends to fill that void and help us bear the grief.

Anytime we face grief, we are in danger of becoming stuck in it and not moving on with our lives after a season of grieving. In *All's Well That Ends Well,* Shakespeare warns that grief can become an enduring obstacle to enjoying life:

> Moderate lamentation is the right of the dead;
> excessive grief the enemy of the living. (Act I, scene i)

He explains in *Macbeth* that "the night is long that never

finds the day." (Act IV, scene iii) Grief can become a long dark night. Like during any sleepless night, during grief we must look for the light and embrace it at dawn, even when we want to stay in bed hiding under the covers.

GUILT: JUST SAY NO!

Guilt can become one of the most destructive spiritual forces in our lives. It functions as a spiritual virus that attacks the mind, emotions and even the body. We can attempt to suppress it, ignore it, or pay for it in various ways, but it works in us and plagues us with anxiety, shame and regret. Sooner or later a person faces his or her guilt and rejects it, confesses and repents of it, or continues to bear it miserably without relief.

There are many murderers in Shakespeare's plays. The murderers often seem to profit from their evil acts without consequence; however, as the plays progress, we see that their guilt indeed arises within them and haunts them while they are awake and asleep.

In *Macbeth*, the murdering Macbeths gain the throne and try to enjoy their ill-gotten gain but are consumed by guilt. After Macbeth kills the king, he fails to smear the guards with the king's blood and plant the dagger in their hands to frame them for the murder. He fears to return to the room as his guilt immediately condemns him. He tells his wife he will not return to look at what he has done. She boldly grabs the knife and, without hesitation, smears the guards with the king's blood and leaves the knife.

Her boldness and lust for power has temporarily suppressed her conscience. She thinks, therefore, she will be immune from guilt. She returns bloody-handed to Macbeth and boasts to him:

> My hands are of your colour; but I shame
> To wear a heart so white...
> A little water clears us of this deed:
> How easy is it, then! (Act II, scene ii)

This statement represents a delusion involving consequences for deeds opposing one's conscience. Because one chooses to overlook conscience and do evil does not mean guilt will be avoided internally or externally.

As Lady Macbeth finds out later in the play, guilt eventually overwhelms a person. The bloody deed that she thought "a little water would clear" stains her conscience despite her obsessive hand-cleansing oblations. It becomes a spot on her soul and spirit and leads to suicide. In the final act of Macbeth, she desperately tries to cleanse her hands repeatedly from the imagined blood of King Duncan. Her words indicate a guilt-induced dementia as she sees the blood of Duncan and relives the murder scene in her mind; yet, she cannot cleanse herself:

> Out, damned spot! out, I say!--One: two: why,
> then, 'tis time to do't.--Hell is murky!--Fie, my
> lord, fie! a soldier, and afeard? What need we
> fear who knows it, when none can call our power to
> account?--Yet who would have thought the old man
> to have had so much blood in him...
> What, will these hands ne'er be clean?--No more o'
> that, my lord, no more o' that: you mar all with
> this starting...
> Here's the smell of the blood still: all the
> perfumes of Arabia will not sweeten this little
> hand. Oh, oh, oh! (Act V, scene i)

Lady Macbeth's guilt causes her to become insane. Her guilt weighs upon her heart, and her outward activities cannot reach into her heart and remove guilt. Her doctor in the play correctly ascertains his inability to help her:

> More needs she the divine than the physician.
> God, God forgive us all! (Act V, scene i)

Unfortunately, neither Macbeth nor his wife turn to God for absolution of their sins, and they perish in states of disorder, anxiety and rage.

In *Hamlet*, Shakespeare shows the intrinsic conflict guilty people experience. Claudius expresses a pang of conscience regarding the murder of his brother and the usurpation of the throne; however, although he is inclined to pray and seek forgiveness from God, he would rather possess the fruits of his crime than give them up in confession of guilt and repentance. He confides to himself,

> O, my offence is rank it smells to heaven;
> It hath the primal eldest curse upon't,
> A brother's murder! Pray can I not,
> Though inclination be as sharp as will:
> My stronger guilt defeats my strong intent;
> And, like a man to double business bound,
> I stand in pause where I shall first begin,
> And both neglect. What if this cursed hand
> Were thicker than itself with brother's blood,
> Is there not rain enough in the sweet heavens
> To wash it white as snow? Whereto serves mercy
> But to confront the visage of offence?
> And what's in prayer but this two-fold force,

> To be forestalled ere we come to fall,
> Or pardon'd being down? Then I'll look up;
> My fault is past. But, O, what form of prayer
> Can serve my turn? 'Forgive me my foul murder'?
> That cannot be; since I am still possest
> Of those effects for which I did the murder,--
> My crown, mine own ambition and my queen. (Act III, scene iii)

Because Claudius covets the crown, power and his queen, he lacks willingness to release these prizes along with his guilt. He refuses to pray and seek forgiveness, though his guilt condemns him. In this soliloquy, Shakespeare also teaches that mercy exists to forgive guilt, "Whereto serves mercy but to confront the visage of offence?" Unlike Claudius, we must take advantage of mercy, or it is useless to us.

Each step of the way in doing evil offers a choice to repentantly face justice and seek mercy or to continue doing evil while attempting to cover one's guilt. Claudius chooses to follow his ambition and devises additional murderous schemes rather than confess his guilt. Even so, eventually his guilt is uncovered by forces he cannot control, and he faces justice, not mercy.

Although he wears religious garb and performs religious duties, Cardinal Beaufort conspires murder in *The Second Part of King Henry the Sixth* and faces judgment for it. His hidden guilt leads him to his deathbed, as an attendant describes:

> Cardinal Beaufort is at point of death;
> For suddenly a grievous sickness took him,
> That makes him gasp and stare and catch the air,
> Blaspheming God and cursing men on earth.

> Sometimes he talks as if Duke Humphrey's ghost
> Were by his side; sometime he calls the king,
> And whispers to his pillow, as to him,
> The secrets of his overcharged soul; (Act III, scene ii)

The Cardinal is a religious person who attempts to turn off his conscience. He learns that it runs on autopilot and still convicts him of his corruption. Cardinal Beaufort's guilt leads him to a terrifying death during which he bargains and pleads for respite from his physical pain and mental torment—both caused by his guilty conscience.

Shakespeare emphatically shows in his plays that the lowly and the mighty cannot escape payment for their guilt—spiritually or physically. The oppressed conscience of King Richard III in *King Richard the Third* even arises as if from death to condemn him. He confesses to himself,

> My conscience hath a thousand several tongues,
> And every tongue brings in a several tale,
> And every tale condemns me for a villain.
> Perjury, perjury, in the high'st degree
> Murder, stem murder, in the direst degree;
> All several sins, all used in each degree,
> Throng to the bar, crying all, Guilty! guilty!
> I shall despair. There is no creature loves me;
> And if I die, no soul shall pity me:
> Nay, wherefore should they, since that I myself
> Find in myself no pity to myself? (Act V, scene iii)

When it is all said and done in Shakespeare's plays and

in life, the prize won immorally pales in comparison with the torment of guilt and suffering that is glimpsed in the guilty person's life and death.

INDIVIDUAL RESPONSIBILITY: PLEASE TAKE IT

Adults are responsible for their spiritual condition and direction. People may try to excuse spiritual laziness, immaturity, or immorality because of how they were raised, abused, neglected, spoiled or tempted, but when it finally comes down to it, each person's spirit, soul and body are his or her own. Some people have had great trials and tortuous pasts worthy of sympathy, but regardless of who we are, where we are, or where we have been, Shakespeare's plays prod us to take ownership of our spirituality.

Shakespeare emphasizes the virtue of individual responsibility in no uncertain terms. In *King Henry the Fifth*, King Henry V, disguised as a common soldier, discusses with some of his soldiers whether the king is responsible for all his soldiers' souls while leading them into battle. King Henry V, Shakespeare's icon of positive spirituality, makes the case that ends the argument:

> the king is not bound to answer the particular end-
> ings of his
> soldiers, the father of his son, nor the master of
> his servant.... Every subject's duty is the king's; but
> every subject's
> soul is his own. Therefore should every soldier in
> the wars do as every sick man in his bed,--wash every

> mote out of his conscience: and dying so, death
> is to him advantage; or not dying, the time was
> blessedly lost wherein such preparation was gained:
> (Act IV, scene i)

Shakespeare encourages every person to examine his or her conscience and to find redemption and peace. We, like a soldier, should not take our days to come for granted. Any time we spend today ministering to the condition of our spirit and soul is "blessedly" spent. No one else can do this work for us.

In Shakespeare's time, as in ours, people have justified not taking responsibility for their spirituality and decisions by assigning responsibility to various entities like the stars and planets, fortune, other people or God. Shakespeare artfully returns the responsibility to the individual.

In *Julius Caesar*, Cassius convinces Brutus to take action regarding their situation in Rome by turning his gaze from fate to himself:

> Men at some time are masters of their fates.
> The fault, dear Brutus, is not in our stars,
> But in ourselves, that we are underlings. (Act I, scene ii)

Cassius could have as easily said to Brutus, "stop complaining about the situation and do something about it!" The reward of individual responsibility is that by accepting it we gain individual power over our lives.

In *Hamlet*, Prince Hamlet hesitates to take the responsibility to mete out justice in his kingdom. When he learns about his father's murder from the ghost of his father, he recognizes his duty but despises it:

SHAKESPEARE ON SPIRITUALITY

> The time is out of joint: O cursed spite,
> That ever I was born to set it right! (Act I, scene v)

Prince Hamlet sort of shirks his responsibility by playing games with Claudius and Polonius. His delay in taking action undermines his purpose and results in tragedy. If he had accepted responsibility immediately, maybe only Claudius would have died. Any delay in accepting responsibility for ourselves and our duty may cause irrevocable damage.

Shakespeare encourages us to take charge of our lives. He indicates that when we accept our responsibilities, we find sufficient resources to overcome problems and trials. Helena, a wise woman in *All's Well that Ends Well,* counsels that we ought to have a solution-oriented attitude towards life's problems:

> Our remedies oft in ourselves do lie,
> Which we ascribe to heaven: the fated sky
> Gives us free scope, only doth backward pull
> Our slow designs when we ourselves are dull. (Act I, scene i)

Shakespeare advises us not to naively wish upon a star or hope in fate. He encourages taking a proactive approach to life.

Likewise, he allows no valid excuse for doing evil. We are responsible for the evil acts we commit, and to take responsibility spiritually is to acknowledge our shortcomings, weaknesses and mistakes. In *King Lear,* Shakespeare illustrates through Edmund, the evil bastard son of King Lear, that there is no excuse for our actions, not fate or the stars, not God, not other people and not circumstances. Edmund explains,

> This is the excellent foppery of the world, that, when we are sick in fortune,--often the surfeit of our own behavior,--we make guilty of our disasters the sun, the moon, and the stars: as if we were villains by necessity; fools by heavenly compulsion; knaves, thieves, and treachers, by spherical predominance; drunkards, liars, and adulterers, by an enforced obedience of planetary influence; and all that we are evil in, by a divine thrusting on: an admirable evasion of whoremaster man, to lay his goatish disposition to the charge of a star! (Act I, scene ii)

Shakespeare uses Edmund's words to confront the irresponsible, evil behavior of people. According to Shakespeare, God has given us the initiative and responsibility to make things happen in our lives. Whether what we have done or where we are in life is good or evil, we have to look inward and ask the question, "What am I going to do about it?"

INTUITION: THE SPIRIT'S VOICE

The idea of women's intuition is cliché in modern times, but to Shakespeare, intuition indicates a person's (male or female) innate ability to ascertain from the universe insights regarding situations, the future or other people. A person's subconscious always works and remains aware of current situations; if the person is spiritually sensitive, his or her consciousness will become informed by the intimations from the subconscious, the heart and from God. Intuition may come in the form of clear expectations or as a sense of foreboding or excitement regarding what is to come. Intuition can stir lifesaving warnings of danger or produce adventurous anticipation. It can also offer discernment regarding important decisions.

Sometimes, a person cannot place the exact reason for intuition's message but recognizes a strong feeling stemming from deep inside. King Richard's Queen in *King Richard the Second* has such an experience as she is separated from the King and suffers a sudden grief without any apparent cause:

> …yet I know no cause
> Why I should welcome such a guest as grief,
> Save bidding farewell to so sweet a guest
> As my sweet Richard: yet again, methinks,
> Some unborn sorrow, ripe in fortune's womb,
> Is coming towards me, and my inward soul

> With nothing trembles: at something it grieves,
> More than with parting from my lord the king. (Act II, scene ii)

The queen's friend Bushy attempts to assuage her grief by persuading her that it is based on something imaginary, but the queen responds to him that "her inward soul" convinces her it is otherwise. The Queen actually senses the circumstances that will lead to the king's overthrow and death.

Intuition is our inner soul discerning something that consciously we do not identify. We are tempted by others and logic to suppress our intuition and deny it as nonsensical.

In *King Richard the Third*, Shakespeare calls intuition a "divine instinct" by which men's minds detect ensuing dangers prior to any apparent indication of change. In *Hamlet*, the good friend Horatio inwardly perceives from recent events something that causes him to expect misfortune for Denmark:

> In what particular thought to work I know not;
> But in the gross and scope of my opinion,
> This bodes some strange eruption to our state. (Act I, scene i)

Horatio attempts to use his intuition and insight to counsel Hamlet in the course of the ensuing events. However, intuition often presents a vague picture of things, and people are rarely quick to trust their instincts or internal counsel. Hamlet demonstrates this as his intuition tells him plainly that the ghost speaks the truth about the murdering Claudius. This is later confirmed by the actions of Claudius, but Hamlet is slow to act on his intuition. We all would benefit from becoming more sensitive to our own "divine instinct."

People will trust the total stranger quicker than they will trust their own intuition. Usually the consequence is minor, but sometimes it is a life and death decision not to follow our intuition. If the question is whether to follow our intuition at the risk of mildly offending a person or appearing foolish, we should always go with our own soul's guidance; after all, our intuition has our best interests in mind.

LOVE OF ALL

Many of Shakespeare's plays center on the theme of love. In certain verses, he speaks particularly of love, but in all of the plays, he illustrates lessons on love. His ideas and wisdom concerning love transcend a single definition. He speaks of romantic love, sacrificial love, love for family, for friends, and for country; he shows pure love and contrasts it with perverted notions of love expressed in jealousy, vanity, selfishness and abuse.

Most importantly, in the plays, Shakespeare shows us how to recognize and express true love. He emphasizes the actions of love. Love is more than words of poetry or seductive promises. Of love, he writes, "it cannot speak; for truth hath better deeds than words to grace it." (*The Two Gentleman of Verona*--Act II, scene ii) Inspiring action in people, love empowers a person to act more nobly and adroitly than before he or she loved. In *Love's Labour's Lost*, the lover Berowne describes the heightening effects of love that give a person increased sensitivity, virtue and power,

> But love, first learned in a lady's eyes,
> Lives not alone immured in the brain;
> But, with the motion of all elements,
> Courses as swift as thought in every power,
> And gives to every power a double power,
> Above their functions and their offices.

> It adds a precious seeing to the eye;
> A lover's eyes will gaze an eagle blind;
> A lover's ear will hear the lowest sound,
> When the suspicious head of theft is stopt:
> Love's feeling is more soft and sensible
> Than are the tender horns of cockled snails;
> Love's tongue proves dainty Bacchus gross in taste:
> For valour, is not Love a Hercules,
> Still climbing trees in the Hesperides?
> Subtle as Sphinx; as sweet and musical
> As bright Apollo's lute, strung with his hair:
> And when Love speaks, the voice of all the gods
> Makes heaven drowsy with the harmony.
> Never durst poet touch a pen to write
> Until his ink were temper'd with Love's sighs;
> O, then his lines would ravish savage ears
> And plant in tyrants mild humility. (Act IV, scene iii)

This commentary on love convinces me that love is the desired state of life in which a person reaches his or her full potential in service to others and experiences all the joys of relationships. We would enjoy our lives more and do more good if we could live under the influence of such love.

The true love that empowers a person is further described by Shakespeare in *As You Like It*. The speaker, Silvius, is in the bliss of romantic love; he explains the essence of true love:

> It is to be all made of sighs and tears;...
> it is to be all made of faith and service;...
> It is to be all made of fantasy,
> All made of passion, and all made of wishes,
> All adoration, duty, and observance,

All humbleness, all patience and impatience,
All purity, all trial, all deservings; (Act V, scene ii)

Love proves itself in actions and character. A true lover does not love to satisfy selfish pleasures but to serve the object of his or her love. The above lines would make a fitting reading at weddings and throughout marriage.

In *King Lear*, King Lear asks his three daughters to tell him how much they love him in order to win from him an inheritance. Two of the daughters proclaim their love in poetic platitudes; however, Cordelia refuses to speak of her love just to gain favor from her father. She tells herself, "I am sure, my love's more richer than my tongue," (Act I, scene i) and then she merely points to her loving actions and her honor of her father. In response, King Lear gives her inheritance to the two sisters who have verbosely sworn love to their father. King Lear decides not to give any inheritance or portion of his kingdom to Cordelia.

Cordelia's suitor of late, the Duke of Burgundy, refuses to marry her without the dowry of her inheritance; he shows that his love is for her fortune. Conversely, the King of France embraces the opportunity to wed Cordelia, even without her dowry. He professes his love to her alone:

> Fairest Cordelia, that art most rich, being poor;
> Most choice, forsaken; and most loved, despised!
> Thee and thy virtues here I seize upon:
> Be it lawful I take up what's cast away.
> Gods, gods! 'tis strange that from their cold'st neglect
> My love should kindle to inflamed respect.
> Thy dowerless daughter, king, thrown to my chance,
> Is queen of us, of ours, and our fair France:

> Not all the dukes of waterish Burgundy
> Can buy this unprized precious maid of me. (Act I, scene i)

In marriage ceremonies, husbands and wives make vows to love during good times and bad times, yet few take into account what bad times may come. At some point, marriages face physical, financial, or emotional adversities. If true love is not the overwhelming motivating reason to marry, then when the idyllic season fades, the commitment to marriage may dissolve in the face of trials. The attitude of the King of France toward marrying Cordelia conveyed in the above passage serves as an example to couples considering marriage, because successful marriage requires two people committed to loving the other under all circumstances.

As Shakespeare teaches in *A Midsummer Night's Dream*, there are obstacles in loving relationships that challenge the love's merit:

> For aught that I could ever read,
> Could ever hear by tale or history,
> The course of true love never did run smooth. (Act I, scene i)

Loving unselfishly is a challenge and a sacrifice. True love is invariably tested, and its worth must be proven.

In *King Lear*, Shakespeare shows us the commitment of a true lover to love a person regardless of circumstances or what one may gain or suffer. The sisters Goneril and Regan, who swear love to their father, soon reject him and cast him out of their lives. Their actions demonstrate the emptiness of words of love without the substance of loving actions and commitment.

As true as this is, we should remember that honest conveyance of our love should not be withheld. Cordeilia could have been more liberal with her declarations of love for her father without compromising the verity of its existence. Love is best expressed when words and actions converge and confirm one another.

Love itself is immeasurable and infinite in source. In *Romeo and Juliet*, love empowers Romeo to scale a wall that he might catch a glimpse of Juliet, and Shakespeare confirms that love can do anything it dares to do. Romeo declares the power of his love to Juliet:

> With love's light wings did I o'er-perch these walls;
> For stony limits cannot hold love out,
> And what love can do that dares love attempt. (Act II, scene i)

Love inspires, motivates, purifies and strengthens a person to perform great and unselfish deeds. One of the primary goals of spirituality should be to love unselfishly, unconditionally and untiringly. In response to Romeo's ferocious love, Juliet answers in equal measure, explaining the infinite bounty of her love:

> My bounty is as boundless as the sea,
> My love as deep; the more I give to thee,
> The more I have, for both are infinite. (Act II, scene i)

I do not presume that Shakespeare equates the romantic love of Romeo and Juliet to true love that lasts a lifetime; however, long-lasting steadfast love cannot begin with a greater spark of excitement than we witness between Romeo and Juliet. They only lacked the wisdom to navigate their families' conflicts.

Spiritually minded people do not place restraints or brakes on love; they love naively and unreservedly. To grow spiritually, we have to become like children in so many ways, and in *The Two Gentlemen of Verona*, Shakespeare tells us that love is also childlike:

> For love is like a child,
> That longs for every thing that he can come by. (Act III, scene i)

The most childlike action we can take in the course of love is to love all that we can find to love and to love purely for love's sake.

LOYALTY IS PRICELESS

When kingdoms, princes, wealth, power, love and ambition are subjects of plays, loyalty of subjects, friends and lovers is constantly a topic on center stage. Shakespeare presents the tension in characters' bosoms between loyalty and selfish desire. Many of Shakespeare's tragedies are defined by disloyalty to king, family or friends.

Whether it is Claudius in *Hamlet*, Macbeth in *Macbeth*, Goneril and Regan in *King Lear*, Brutus and Cassius in *Julius Caesar*, or Enorbarbus in *Antony and Cleopatra*, the act of betrayal marks the downward spiral toward tragedy.

Conversely, the virtue of loyalty in a character conveys a redemptive quality to the audience or reader of the plays. The loyalty of men like Gloster, Bedford, Exeter, Westmoreland, Erpingham and Fluellen to King Henry V in *King Henry the Fifth* balances the dark betrayals to King Henry V by Cambridge, Scroop and Grey.

The Duke of Gloster, brother to King Henry V and uncle to King Henry VI, demonstrates continued loyalty in *The Second Part of King Henry VI* to the young child-king of whom he is guardian and protector. Gloster is prodded by his wife to pursue the crown from King Henry VI. Although he is in a position from which he could coercively gain the crown, Gloster admirably defends his loyalty to King Henry VI and rebukes his wife:

> O Nell, sweet Nell, if thou dost love thy lord,
> Banish the canker of ambitious thoughts!
> And may that thought, when I imagine ill
> Against my king and nephew, virtuous Henry,
> Be my last breathing in this mortal world!...
> Presumptuous dame, ill-nurtured Eleanor,
> Art thou not second woman in the realm,
> And the Protector's wife, beloved of him?
> Hast thou not worldly pleasure at command,
> Above the reach or compass of thy thought?
> And wilt thou still be hammering treachery,
> To tumble down thy husband and thyself
> From top of honour to disgrace's feet?
> Away from me, and let me hear no more! (Act I, scene i)

Gloster shows us how to respond to temptations of betrayal. Nothing we gain in this world will accompany us to the next except the relationships we have developed. To sacrifice an eternal friendship and trust for the sake of worldly gain, a person demonstrates a lack of spiritual understanding and discipline. Due to his integrity, Gloster does not even consider his wife's suggestions.

In *The Two Gentleman of Verona,* Proteus faces severe conviction from his conscience when his betrayal of his best friend Valentine is exposed. He pinpoints man's inability to remain loyal as the chief cause of downfall:

> ...'tis true. O heaven! were man
> But constant, he were perfect! That one error
> Fills him with faults; makes him run through all the sins:
> Inconstancy falls off ere it begins. (Act V, scene iv)

If a person remains loyal in relationships, many other personal qualities fall into line; however, we find ourselves continually tempted to let others down rather than sacrificing a want or convenience. Proteus pursues a sexual attraction to Valentine's girlfriend rather than stand true to his friendship.

We should strive to possess more determination and passion regarding our loyalty. Several of Shakespeare's characters would sooner forfeit their lives than their loyalty. In *King Richard the Second*, the Duke of Norfolk defends his loyalty to King Richard II as the badge of his honor:

> My dear dear lord,
> The purest treasure mortal times afford
> Is spotless reputation: that away,
> Men are but gilded loam or painted clay.
> A jewel in a ten-times-barr'd-up chest
> Is a bold spirit in a loyal breast.
> Mine honour is my life; both grow in one:
> Take honour from me, and my life is done:
> Then, dear my liege, mine honour let me try;
> In that I live and for that will I die. (Act I, scene i)

Norfolk earnestly makes known his willingness to risk his life in a duel against Henry Bolingbroke to prove his loyalty and honor. He later puts his life at risk and willingly wagers his eternity on his loyalty:

> If ever I were a traitor,
> My name be blotted from the book of life,
> And I from heaven banisht as from hence! (Act I, scene iii)

Loyalty is not only key to the success of personal relationships, it is key to the general health and strength of countries, as well as to organizations such as corporations, churches, sports teams, etc. For a nation or group to remain vibrant, members must remain loyal to the overall mission and to each other.

Shakespeare emphasizes the significance of loyalty to the power and self-determination of the nation of England. Following years of civil wars and wars with France described in *King John*, Philip Faulconbridge, the son to Richard I, states that the presence of loyal English Lords is necessary for England to become healthy and remain strong:

> O, let us pay the time but needful woe,
> Since it hath been beforehand with our griefs.
> This England never did, nor never shall,
> Lie at the proud foot of a conqueror,
> But when it first did help to wound itself.
> Now these her princes are come home again,
> Come the three corners of the world in arms,
> And we shall shock them; naught shall make us rue,
> If England to itself do rest but true. (Act V, scene v)

Any group of people committed to one another toward a specific goal can become a force to be reckoned with in any sphere of influence—whether internationally or in a local community; however, if disloyalty seeps into the group, the very infrastructure breaks down, and the organization is threatened with failure and destruction.

Even thieves must have loyalty in their clans. In *The First Part of Henry the Fourth*, the vagabond thief Falstaff laments betrayal by his fellow robbers:

> A plague upon't,
> When thieves cannot be true one to another! (Act II, scene ii)

If loyalty is expected from thieves, surely we who desire to live honorable lives should expect no less from ourselves.

Lovers, like soldiers, must exhibit loyalty to the objects of their affections to build a strong and lasting relationship. When lovers take vows in marriage, their true claim is to remain loyal until death. In an exchange between Hermia and Lysander, two lovers in *A Midsummer Night's Dream,* Shakespeare summarizes the essence and importance of loyalty between lovers*:*

> **HERMIA**
> So far be distant; and, good night, sweet friend:
> Thy love ne'er alter till thy sweet life end!
>
> **LYSANDER**
> Amen, amen, to that fair prayer, say I;
> And then end life when I end loyalty! (Act II, scene ii)

Unfortunately, many spouses end loyalty when it loses its appeal. The high divorce rate in the United States indicates that loyalty is an endangered virtue among spouses. Loyalty must be one of the chief aims in a happy marriage.

Shakespeare strongly condemns disloyalty. An example showing his attitude toward betrayers is found in *Timon of Athens.* Timon who has generously lent money to his friends finds himself without means to support his estate. When he sends his servant Falminius to his friend Lucullus for recompense of favors and money that had been given to him by Timon, Flaminius is coldly rebuked, and Lucullus mocks Timon. Flaminius recognizes the betrayal and speaks sharply against Lucullus:

> Let moulten coin be thy damnation,
> Thou disease of a friend, and not himself!
> Has friendship such a faint and milky heart,
> It turns in less than two nights? O you gods,
> I feel my master's passion! this slave,
> Unto dishonour, has my lord's meat in him:
> Why should it thrive and turn to nutriment,
> When he is turn'd to poison?
> O, may diseases only work upon't!
> And, when he's sick to death, let not that part of nature
> Which my lord paid for, be of any power
> To expel sickness, but prolong his hour! (Act III, scene i)

As a response to and result of the disloyalty of those who had seemed friends to Timon, Timon retreats from his estate and dies as a poor recluse. This play is a clear indictment of disloyalty to friends in need. Loyalty is only tested when it is inconvenient and costly. If it does not prove its merit during such tests, it lacks the true substance required of friendship.

In *Antony and Cleopatra*, Antony's fellow soldier and friend Enorbarbus abandons Antony following an apparent defeat in battle by Octavius Caesar's forces. Enorbarbus, against the instruction of his heart, deserts to the side he perceives as the likely victor. His heart indicts him for his dishonor in desertion of Antony, and in his final soliloquy, he convicts himself of his guilt:

> O sovereign mistress of true melancholy,
> The poisonous damp of night disponge upon me,
> That life, a very rebel to my will,
> May hang no longer on me: throw my heart
> Against the flint and hardness of my fault:
> Which, being dried with grief, will break to powder,
> And finish all foul thoughts. O Antony,
> Nobler than my revolt is infamous,
> Forgive me in thine own particular;
> But let the world rank me in register
> A master-leaver and a fugitive
> O Antony! O Antony! (Act IV, scene ix)

Enorbarbus' guilt at his disloyalty condemns him to die of a broken and shamed heart. Certainly, he wishes he had clung to Antony, even in defeat, rather than attempting to save himself with desertion.

When someone is disloyal to us, it hurts our heart and soul and can cause us to lower our regard of the whole of humanity. Shakespeare's Henry V responds to the betrayal of his three advisors and nobles as if their treason created a blot on all of those around him. In *King Henry the Fifth*, the King rates the injury caused by his three betrayers and would-be assassins:

> Thy fall hath left a kind of blot,
> To mark the full-fraught man and best indued
> With some suspicion. I will weep for thee;
> For this revolt of thine, methinks, is like
> Another fall of man. (Act II, scene ii)

If those you loved and trusted have betrayed you, then you know Shakespeare's estimation of the pain and severity of disloyalty is not an exaggeration.

It would be a great comment on the blessedness of our lives if, at the end, we can say as Brutus does in *Julius Caesar* when he prepares to run onto his sword:

> My heart doth joy, that yet, in all my life,
> I found no man but he was true to me. (Act V, scene v)

Along with the hope that people will be true to us, we can find few, if any, spiritual pursuits more worthwhile than striving to be found loyal in all of our relationships.

MARRIAGE VOWS

Besides the relationship with God, perhaps no relationship is as important to an adult as the marriage relationship. In many ways, the health of a marriage correlates strongly to the spiritual health of both spouses. Spousal relationships are like extensions of self. A discussion of spirituality is incomplete without offering insights and wisdom about marriage and its spiritual qualities.

The spirituality of marriage begins with vows, prayers and the coming together of two spiritual beings. A healthy marriage is dependent upon the equitable contributions of two mature people. One person can be responsible for his or her spirituality and health but not for the health of a marriage as a whole—that requires the work of both spouses.

Shakespeare recognizes the importance of marriage to fulfilling the human experience and incorporates profundities concerning marriage throughout his plays. In *The First Part of King Henry the Sixth*, he relates a view on methods for choosing a spouse. The Earl of Suffolk, who is trying to influence the King in choosing who to marry, explains the benefits of avoiding an arranged marriage in favor of marrying for love,

> For what is wedlock forced but a hell,
> An age of discord and continual strife?
> Whereas the contrary bringeth bliss,
> And is a pattern of celestial peace. (Act V, scene v)

Surely, you and people you know would not submit to prearranged marriages in our times; however, people today may seek to marry because they feel pressure from family, friends or themselves to "get married." The opinions of others, fear of being alone, insecurity or unfulfilled expectations can play the role of dictators in our lives. In any of our decisions, especially in choosing who and when to marry, we are most fulfilled when we choose for positive reasons such as love rather than negative ones like fear or desperation.

Shakespeare also counsels against rushing into marriage. He writes in *The Third Part of King Henry the Sixth,* "Hasty marriage seldom proveth well." (Act IV, scene i) However, as we know, when someone is smitten, he or she wants to marry and does not listen to counsel urging against it. Benedick, in *Much Ado about Nothing,* is a committed bachelor until he falls in love and drastically changes his tune:

> In brief, since I do purpose to marry,
> I will think nothing to any purpose
> that the world can say against it. (Act V, scene iv)

The term "madly in love" is apropos to Benedick and to many people who meet someone and rush into marriage. One must remember that romantic feelings are fleeting, but true love perseveres through hardships and importunities.

In *The Second Part of King Henry the Sixth,* King Henry VI approaches marriage with the beneficial attitude. Even though he has not previously met his soon-to-be-wife, he greets her with a kiss, a prayer and a compliment:

> Welcome, Queen Margaret:
> I can express no kinder sign of love

> Than this kind kiss.—O Lord, that lends me life,
> Lend me a heart replete with thankfulness!
> For Thou has given me, in this beauteous face,
> A world of earthly blessings to my soul,
> If sympathy of love unite our thoughts. (Act I, scene i)

This same attitude should bless our marriages, and they would undoubtedly be more successful if, like King Henry VI in the above excerpt, we would maintain kindness, thankfulness, love for one another and would begin conversations with kisses and compliments.

In *King Henry the Fifth,* Queen Isabella of France prays a blessing over the union of King Henry V of England and her daughter Katherine that provides several keys to a blissful marriage:

> God, the best maker of all marriages,
> Combine your hearts in one, your realms in one!
> As man and wife, being two, are one in love,
> So be there 'twixt your kingdoms such a spousal,
> That never may ill office, or fell jealousy,
> Which troubles oft the bed of blessed marriage,
> Thrust in between the paction of these kingdoms,
> To make divorce of their incorporate league;
> That English may as French, French Englishmen,
> Receive each other! God speak this Amen! (Act V, scene ii)

Shakespeare writes that God can melt the hearts of lovers as one and make the two people one in love, trust, family and purpose. Marriage too often consists of two people living under the same roof but maintaining separate lives.

Shakespeare shares the truth that marriage involves union and submission to each other and fortification against the enemies of marriage.

There is no treatise on marriage in Shakespeare's plays like the presentation of marriage in *The Taming of the Shrew.* Certainly, the culture of Shakespeare's times was much different from ours. In his time, husbands and wives assumed roles in marriages that are not what we expect in our marriages. Even so, in *The Taming of the Shrew,* Shakespeare illustrates the spirit of a healthy marriage that can be adopted by husbands and wives today. It is a spirit of mutual respect, service, humility, love and care. It is the spirit and attitude finally adopted by Katharina (the shrew) as she describes to other wives her ideas of a wife's proper attitude toward her husband. If we overlook the outdated roles she describes, we can identify true spousal love and respect that forms the heart of a strong marriage:

> To wound thy lord, thy king, thy governor:
> It blots thy beauty as frosts do bite the meads,
> Confounds thy fame as whirlwinds shake fair buds,
> And in no sense is meet or amiable.
> A woman moved is like a fountain troubled,
> Muddy, ill-seeming, thick, bereft of beauty;
> And while it is so, none so dry or thirsty
> Will deign to sip or touch one drop of it.
> Thy husband is thy lord, thy life, thy keeper,
> Thy head, thy sovereign; one that cares for thee,
> And for thy maintenance commits his body
> To painful labour both by sea and land,
> To watch the night in storms, the day in cold,
> Whilst thou liest warm at home, secure and safe;
> And craves no other tribute at thy hands

> But love, fair looks and true obedience,--
> Too little payment for so great a debt.
> Such duty as the subject owes the prince
> Even such a woman oweth to her husband;
> And when she is froward, peevish, sullen, sour,
> And not obedient to his honest will,
> What is she but a foul contending rebel
> And graceless traitor to her loving lord?
> I am ashamed that women are so simple
> To offer war where they should kneel for peace;
> Or seek for rule, supremacy and sway,
> When they are bound to serve, love and obey. (Act V, scene ii)

In our marriages, husbands and wives play somewhat equal roles and take on shared family and household duties. Rather than dismiss the above admonitions as outdated for wives, I suggest that what is outdated is the application of the above verses only to wives. Husbands, as well as wives, would make strides toward a happy marriage if they would take up the vow to serve, love and obey and not to posture themselves to gain supremacy over their partners. The attitude of love, service and humility described in the above verses contributes to a happy marriage for husbands and wives.

Perhaps the strongest message regarding marriage that comes to us in Shakespeare's plays is the idea that husbands and wives serve each other as supporters, counselors and advisors. In the plays, husbands suffer for not soliciting or accepting their wives' wise counsel regarding decisions. When given, the women's insights often fall on deaf ears and gain mere placating responses.

Lady Percy, in *The First Part of King Henry the Fourth*,

recognizes her husband's withdrawal over some great turmoil and seeks to aid in his burdens. She protests his privations:

> O, my good lord, why are you thus alone?
> For what offence have I this fortnight been
> A banish'd woman from my Harry's bed?
> Tell me, sweet lord, what is't that takes from thee
> Thy stomach, pleasure and thy golden sleep?...
> O, what portents are these?
> Some heavy business hath my lord in hand,
> And I must know it, else he loves me not. (Act II, scene iii)

Like the typical male, instead of sharing what is on his mind with his wife, Hotspur (Henry Percy) jumps on his horse and rides away. Today husbands don't ride off on a horse (probably due only to the lack of an available horse), but we often isolate ourselves or disappear in other ways and fail to communicate our troubles to someone who cares—just like Hotspur in the above scenario and like Brutus in *Julius Caesar*.

The famous traitor Brutus keeps his wife from his most troubling thoughts. Men consistently underestimate their wives' intuition concerning their state of mind and level of contentment. Women know when things are awry, and they possess this gift to help and support their husbands; however, husbands stupidly reject feminine counsel and opt to learn the hard way. The trouble with this path in Shakespeare's plays is that the hard way is usually death.

Brutus is struggling over whether he should join the conspirators when his wife Portia approaches him and offers support:

> My Brutus;
> You have some sick offence within your mind,
> Which, by the right and virtue of my place,
> I ought to know of: and, upon my knees,
> I charm you, by my once-commended beauty,
> By all your vows of love and that great vow
> Which did incorporate and make us one,
> That you unfold to me, yourself, your half,
> Why you are heavy, and what men to-night
> Have had to resort to you: for here have been
> Some six or seven, who did hide their faces
> Even from darkness...
> Within the bond of marriage, tell me, Brutus,
> Is it excepted I should know no secrets
> That appertain to you? Am I yourself
> But, as it were, in sort or limitation,
> To keep with you at meals, comfort your bed,
> And talk to you sometimes? Dwell I but in the suburbs
> Of your good pleasure? If it be no more,
> Portia is Brutus' harlot, not his wife. (Act II, scene i)

Brutus refuses to allow his wife into his private thoughts and instead joins the conspirators and becomes a renowned traitor. His treachery leads to his death and Portia's suicide. What trials and mistakes could men avoid if they would listen to their wives' counsel? Spouses are blessed to have a companion to share burdens and delights, but too often both husbands and wives disconnect from one another and try to carry their burdens alone, thus they undercut the foundation of the marriage.

MERCY ME

Mercy plays a vital role in healthy spirituality. We need mercy from God and mercy from others, and our need to grant mercy equals both of these. No relationship can remain healthy without the free and frequent give and take of mercy and forgiveness. None of us can even approach a relationship with God without receiving a constant flow of his mercy.

Shakespeare recognizes and artfully presents the cycle of mercy that is the life-flow of the spirituality present in his plays. The cycle begins with God, the only perfect one, forgiving people, as Isabella argues in *Measure for Measure*, a play that centers on mercy:

> Why, all the souls that were were forfeit once;
> And He that might the vantage best have took
> Found out the remedy. How would you be,
> If He, which is the top of judgment, should
> But judge you as you are? O, think on that;
> And mercy then will breathe within your lips,
> Like man new-made. (Act II, scene ii)

In *Measure for Measure,* as the title implies and as demonstrated in the above quote, Shakespeare explains that we need mercy and should therefore give mercy. The downside to this scenario is that when people do not give mercy they also fail to receive mercy when they need it, and so rather than two parties gaining blessings, the two parties gain judgment and condemnation.

The severest example of this sowing and reaping is seen in *King Henry the Fifth.* King Henry and his nobles, along with his army, are preparing to sail for France to fight for his right to the French throne. Prior to sailing, King Henry discusses the consequences for an arrested English citizen who railed against him the previous day. King Henry pardons him mercifully and commands his release. Three of his noble advisors argue that the man should be punished and then released, because after all, "you show great mercy, if you give him life, after the taste of much correction," they argue. (Act II, scene ii) The king follows the course of mercy and releases the man unpunished.

Unfortunately, for the three who advise punishment, it has been found out that they are traitors planning to betray King Henry and England. When confronted, they all beg for mercy, but as they find out from the King, they did not offer mercy to the man who had railed against the king, so they shall receive no mercy. The King promptly rebukes their pleas for mercy:

> The mercy that was quick in us but late,
> By your own counsel is supprest and kill'd:
> You must not dare, for shame, to talk of mercy;
> For your own reasons turn into your bosoms,
> As dogs upon their masters, worrying you. (Act II,
>   scene ii)

Ouch! We should be careful how we deal with other persons' faults and wrongs, because our own will one day have to be dealt with too. If we want mercy, we must first give it. King Henry sentences these betrayers to death.

SHAKESPEARE ON SPIRITUALITY

In *The Merchant of Venice,* Shakespeare reaches the highest of spiritual heights in his description of mercy through Portia in the court of Venice. On behalf of Bassanio, she argues for mercy from the moneylender Shylock who demands his literal "pound of flesh" in repayment for an overdue debt:

> The quality of mercy is not strain'd,
> It droppeth as the gentle rain from heaven
> Upon the place beneath: it is twice blest;
> It blesseth him that gives and him that takes:
> 'Tis mightiest in the mightiest: it becomes
> The thronèd monarch better than his crown;
> His sceptre shows the force of temporal power,
> The attribute to awe and majesty,
> Wherein doth sit the dread and fear of kings;
> But mercy is above this sceptred sway;
> It is enthroned in the hearts of kings,
> It is an attribute to God himself;
> And earthly power doth then show likest God's
> When mercy seasons justice. Therefore, Jew,
> Though justice be thy plea, consider this,
> That, in the course of justice, none of us
> Should see salvation: we do pray for mercy;
> And that same prayer doth teach us all to render
> The deeds of mercy. (Act IV, scene i)

This speech captures the entire cycle and substance of mercy; nothing needs to be added to it. We could benefit by repeating it daily that we might live by it.

Shakespeare states elsewhere that mercy is indeed the virtue of greatness. "Sweet mercy is nobility's true badge," he writes in *Titus Andronicus,* which is ironically a tragedy that lacks mercy and portrays instead a circle of violence. In *Measure for Measure*, he again writes of mercy through the character Isabella who ascribes mercy to great people:

> Well, believe this,
> No ceremony that to great ones 'longs,
> Not the king's crown nor the deputed sword,
> The marshal's truncheon nor the judge's robe,
> Become them with one half so good a grace
> As mercy does. (Act II, scene ii)

Shakespeare argues that to be great one must be merciful and that no attribute adorns the great like mercy does.

In *King Henry the Eighth,* the Duke of Buckingham, on his way to his execution, demonstrates the attitude of healthy spirituality when he is asked by another man for forgiveness for wrongs the man has done to him. He responds,

> I as free forgive you
> As I would be forgiven: I forgive all. (Act II, scene i)

As those who have sinned against God and man, we have no right to withhold mercy from others. When we are unmerciful to others, we are really holding ourselves in judgment.

Lastly, in the cycle of mercy, we must show mercy to ourselves. Shakespeare is not mute regarding the self and the relationship each of us has with our self. He writes in *The Winter's Tale*,

> Do as the heavens have done, forget your evil;
> With them, forgive yourself. (Act V, scene i)

Although we may possess a merciful attitude toward others, sometimes we still keep a record of our sins and continually judge ourselves according to our mistakes, stupid decisions, shortcomings and all the awful things we have done. As God forgives us, we must also forgive us—that means being merciful to ourselves and not punishing ourselves any longer but rather letting go of all of our sins and accepting ourselves lovingly.

PRAYER CHANGES EVERYTHING

Our life emanates from God, and our connection to him determines our spiritual condition and direction. Prayer describes communication with God in myriad forms. We pray with our spoken words, thoughts, songs, and writing. Even when our minds are quiet, the desires of our hearts may rise to Heaven in the most spontaneous of prayers.

In Shakespeare's plays, we see examples of prayers and discussions of prayers. We also see the attitudes of people while in prayer: the good and the bad. Shakespeare teaches the requisites of meaningful prayer: faith, discipline, humility, reverence, sacrifice and passion.

Some of Shakespeare's characters have trouble focusing their minds on God when they try to pray. Their minds are racing with anxieties and distractions. Although they speak as if speaking to God, no connection exists between them and God. Claudius, the murdering brother and king in *Hamlet,* assumes the posture of prayer and attempts to pray but soon learns that he lacks willingness to submit to and trust in God. He describes the results:

> My words fly up, my thoughts remain below:
> Words without thoughts never to heaven go. (Act III, Scene iii)

His religious form and appearance lacks substance and

therefore lacks results. Prayer is an act of acknowledging God's sovereignty. In the process, we must submit ourselves to him which means relinquishing a measure of control in our lives—the very thing Claudius refuses to give up to God.

In *Measure for Measure,* Angelo, the Deputy to the Duke, attempts to pray, but his lustful thoughts regarding the virtuous Isabella prevail in his mind, because they are stronger than his desire for prayer:

> When I would pray and think, I think and pray
> To several subjects. Heaven hath my empty words;
> Whilst my invention, hearing not my tongue,
> Anchors on Isabel: Heaven in my mouth,
> As if I did but only chew his name;
> And in my heart the strong and swelling evil
> Of my conception. (Act II, scene iii)

Some people follow religious norms not in pursuit of God but to satisfy willful desires. Thoughts, like Angelo's, of satisfying selfish desires can consume people and prevent them from offering themselves to God in prayer.

Similarly, anxieties and fears can burden our minds so much that we cannot pray. The remedy is to make our desire to communicate with God outweigh the distractions within our minds and in our environment. This is also true in our communications with people. We cannot connect with them in a significant way when our minds are elsewhere.

Prayer includes making requests to God in hope of gaining his divine intervention, but that is not all that prayer is. In one sense, prayer is a dying to one's own will to live according to God's will and interests. In *Macbeth*, Macduff praises the slain king Duncan and his wife to their son Malcolm. His praise of the queen focuses on her habit of selfless prayer:

> Thy royal father
> Was a most sainted king: the queen that bore thee,
> Oftener upon her knees than on her feet,
> Died every day she lived. (Act IV, scene iii)

Partitioning ourselves in solitude away from the world so we can pray is the suffering of prayer, but this sacrifice can pale in comparison to the joyous life found in communion with God in prayer. If we make a habit of true prayer, in time, we will find ourselves looking forward with excitement to the next time we can spend prayerfully with God.

Through Shakespeare's discussions of prayer, we learn that the main mistake we can make in prayer is failing to be fully present and responsive to God.

Another mistake we can make in prayer is underestimating the power of God. He created all things; he is powerful. The following prayer of Pericles in *Pericles* illustrates God's grandeur. Pericles asks God to calm a threatening storm:

> Thou god of this great vast, rebuke these surges,
> Which wash both heaven and hell; and thou, that hast
> Upon the winds command, bind them in brass,
> Having call'd them from the deep! O, still
> Thy deafening, dreadful thunders; gently quench
> Thy nimble, sulphurous flashes! (Act III, scene i)

God can do anything. In prayer, we must remember God's greatness and trust him to hear and answer our prayers graciously. Not only is he powerful, he is the gentle and loving "widow's champion and defense." (*King Richard the Second*--Act I, scene ii)

Prayers may consist of requests, confessions, sharing thoughts and emotions, praising and worshipping God, or listening to God. Shakespeare advises that even when we pray for things that are not in our overall best interest, God cares for us by withholding our requests:

> We, ignorant of ourselves,
> Beg often our own harms, which the wise powers
> Deny us for our good; so find we profit
> By losing of our prayers (*Antony and Cleopatra*--Act II, scene i)

God answers prayers according to his wisdom, not ours. Let us humbly, expectantly and habitually go to him.

PRIDE COMES BEFORE A FALL

Cause and effect in spirituality is most apparent in the correlation between the vice of pride and an associated downfall. Shakespeare's lessons in spirituality include keen insights teaching the negativities of pride. There are few things that turn others off to a person like pride, yet it exists seemingly unnoticed by those that grant it safe harbor in themselves.

In *King Richard the Second*, King Richard proclaims that "pride must have a fall." (Act V, scene v) This truth is undisputed, but what is disputed or avoided by people is whether they are prideful. We may argue that we do not possess pride, but by making such a claim do we prove that indeed we are prideful? Shakespeare argues through the Princess in *Love's Labour's Lost* that "all pride is willing pride." (Act II, scene i) The honest and wise person examines himself, identifies pride, and seeks a more humble attitude.

In this context, pride is equated to arrogance or conceit. Such pride is not equivalent to a healthy self-esteem, confidence or love for oneself; instead, this pride is a bloated measure of oneself—a measure based on illusion rather than substance. Pride often displays itself in praises and boasts of one's abilities or accomplishments. For example, in *The Second Part of King Henry the Sixth*, the Duke of Suffolk rightly discerns that "small things make base men proud." (Act VI, scene i) Many things that create selfish pride are small and even insignificant in the scheme of life.

Things that fuel pride can often be lost in an instant. Pride is based on illusion, because, at the very least, its basis becomes as nothing in the day of our death. The reasons for pride—wealth, status, beauty, power or glory—do not last forever but dissipate over time, long or short.

Similarly, humility does not mean self-abasement or self-deprecation. Humility is merely an honest examination of self and an unpretentious, assured attitude. Shakespeare reminds us that "self-love is not so vile a sin as self-neglecting." (*King Henry the Fifth*--Act II, scene iv) Having love and care for oneself is a necessary ingredient to healthy spirituality. Poor self-esteem is not the answer to curing pride; rather, self-assurance and self-acceptance prevent pride from creeping up.

The downfall of Julius Caesar, depicted in *Julius Caesar*, illustrates the detrimental effects of pride on an individual. Caesar is a great man, a conqueror and leader. Unfortunately, he puffs himself up so much that he imagines himself as something greater than other men and as immune to what dangers "lesser" men may face. He deceives himself; although he is deaf in one ear and suffers seizures, he perceives himself as beyond vulnerability.

This illusion causes him to ignore warnings of impending betrayal, and he walks into his murder. A discerning and humble person pays attention to intuition and warning signs of danger. Caesar discerns danger signs from Cassius, the leader of the conspirators, but sees himself as beyond impeachment by mere men:

> Yond Cassius has a lean and hungry look;
> He thinks too much: such men are dangerous...
> Would he were fatter! But I fear him not:
> Yet if my name were liable to fear,

> I do not know the man I should avoid
> So soon as that spare Cassius....
> I rather tell thee what is to be fear'd
> Than what I fear,--for always I am Caesar. (Act I, scene ii)

Caesar would have been wise to guard himself against Cassius, but his pride gives him a false sense of security.

His pride later causes him to ignore his wife's portentous dreams and the counsel of his prophets. All warn him not to venture to the senate on the day his betrayers choose to murder him. How does he answer these warnings? By exalting himself above other men, he rebukes intuition, caution and prudence:

> Danger knows full well
> That Caesar is more dangerous than he:
> We are two lions litter'd in one day,
> And I the elder and more terrible:--
> And Caesar shall go forth. (Act II, scene ii)

Caesar mistakenly equates caution with fear and prudence with cowardice. He does indeed go forth and meet his brother, "Danger," and is killed. In Caesar's character, Shakespeare demonstrates the cause and effect of pride; it leads to a downfall.

Pride can be especially subtle. Surely, Caesar deserves to feel proud. After all, he is a great, brave conqueror for Rome, but Shakespeare shows us that to laud our own accomplishments and to praise ourselves undermines the good we have done:

> He that is proud eats up himself; pride
> is his own glass, his own trumpet, his own

chronicle; and whatever praises itself but in the
deed, devours the deed in the praise.
(*Troilus and Cressida*--Act II, scene iii)

When we praise our own actions to others, we negate our good accomplishments in their eyes.

Shakespeare teaches that people abhor the company of the prideful. He also illustrates that pride is not hidden; people can spot it like a black mark upon our countenance. In *Coriolanus*, pride taints a man's honours and causes him to lose favor with others:

> He could not
> Carry his honours even: whether 'twas pride,
> Which out of daily fortune ever taints
> The happy man. (Act IV, scene vii)

No matter how much success or happiness a person enjoys, pride will drive people away. It is not an attribute of the spiritually healthy.

We learn from *King Henry the Eighth* that pride does not come from heaven but from hell. Several of the king's nobles are discussing the hypocritical, prideful Cardinal of York:

> I cannot tell
> What heaven hath given him,--let some graver eye
> Pierce into that; but I can see his pride
> Peep through each part of him: whence has he that?
> If not from hell, the devil is a niggard;
> Or has given all before, and he begins
> A new hell in himself. (Act I, scene i)

As Shakespeare suggests in the verse above, pride is an initial building block of hell. We should avoid, at all cost, anything that comes from hell. Nothing to which we might cling can be more harmful to our spirituality and relationships than pride. We should examine ourselves for pride as if we are a surgeon searching for a cancerous cell, which, if found, is cut out in full.

PROVIDENCE ALONG THE WAY

Providence describes God's movement on our behalf, his care for us and his love for us. Shakespeare's plays present a belief in God's active presence in our lives.

Hamlet is a character familiar with mystery, doubt and indecision, but in the midst of the turmoil described in *Hamlet,* he demonstrates a firm belief in God's participation in the lives of people. Hamlet speaks of a greater purpose that often prevails in life's events:

> Our indiscretion sometime serves us well,
> When our deep plots do pall: and that should learn us
> There's a divinity that shapes our ends,
> Rough-hew them how we will. (Act V, scene ii)

Hamlet later boosts his hope amidst his portentous thoughts by reminding Horatio and himself of God's care for people. "There's a special providence in the fall of a sparrow," he tells Horatio.

Shakespeare restates the idea in *As You Like It* by describing God as "He that doth the ravens feed" and as the one who "providently caters for the sparrow." (Act II, scene iii) If God cares for the ravens and the sparrows, he surely cares more earnestly for people made in his image.

Within God's providence, we often experience struggle after struggle as we strive toward our goals and the fulfillment of dreams. In addition to facing the day-to-day trials that occur, we feel sometimes as though God thwarts our best attempts at doing good rather than helping us reach our goals. Shakespeare teaches, through the god Jupiter in *Cymbeline,* that these obstacles are placed in our way for our ultimate good and actually flow from God's love not punishment or spite:

> Whom best I love I cross; to make my gift,
> The more delay'd, delighted. Be content; (Act V, scene iv)

This truth can encourage us when we face discouragement and disillusionment. It promises reward if we patiently persevere through trials to win the prize we desire. If we do so, we are sure to reap the blessings of providence in our lives as Shakespeare's observes in *King John:*

> When Fortune means to men most good,
> She looks upon them with a threatening eye. (Act III, scene iv)

During the events of our lives, it may be most dark immediately before the light breaks. The thrust of providential thinking is that God is on our side and working for our good—even when we do not perceive it.

We can trust in providence; as Shakespeare writes, "Fortune brings in some boats that are not steered." (*Cymbeline*--Act IV, scene iii) In such cases, the Creator omnipotently steers our vessel. Divine guidance sometimes leads us through the darkness of the unknown. We are reminded that God can see all of the shores, rocks, waves and storms in our path, and he willingly guides us from a higher and more powerful vantage point.

REFORMATION OF THE SOUL

At some point in their lives, people must come to grips with the temptations they face and the evil to which they have succumbed. Gluttony, lust, coveting, conceit, laziness, stealing, drunkenness, sexual immorality, racism, etc. are ever-present temptations in our culture. Shakespeare's plays promote reformation and turning from evil to the pursuit of spirituality based on love and goodness. Through this process, we can reach our full potential as positive and creative people. He also guides us to accept those who are reformed from unpleasant pasts.

I think the most instructive lesson in personal reformation in Shakespeare's plays is the growth of Prince Henry (also referred to as Hal or Harry) who becomes King Henry V. We see his growth from immaturity to maturity in three of the historical plays. Shakespeare introduces us to Prince Henry in *The First Part of King Henry the Fourth*. King Henry IV laments that his son behaves prodigiously while Henry Percy, the son of the Earl of Northumberland, engages in noble pursuits at his father's side:

> Yea, there thou makest me sad and makest me sin
> In envy that my Lord Northumberland
> Should be the father to so blest a son,
> A son who is the theme of honour's tongue;
> Amongst a grove, the very straightest plant;

> Who is sweet Fortune's minion and her pride:
> Whilst I, by looking on the praise of him,
> See riot and dishonour stain the brow
> Of my young Harry. (Act I, scene i)

Henry IV describes his son, Prince Henry, as one who is riotous and dishonorable. He is essentially an embarrassment to his father, the king.

In the next scene, we see Prince Henry involved in debauchery with the miscreant Falstaff in a London tavern. He seems oblivious to his stature as the Prince of Wales, the next in line to the throne; however, we learn that within him is the divine spark of his calling foreshadowing his coming reformation and rise to honor. Alone in the tavern, he speaks of himself regarding his current surroundings, cohorts and his destiny:

> I know you all, and will awhile uphold
> The unyoked humour of your idleness:
> Yet herein will I imitate the sun,
> Who doth permit the base contagious clouds
> To smother up his beauty from the world,
> That, when he please again to be himself,
> Being wanted, he may be more wonder'd at,
> By breaking through the foul and ugly mists
> Of vapours that did seem to strangle him.
> If all the year were playing holidays,
> To sport would be as tedious as to work;
> But when they seldom come, they wish'd for come,
> And nothing pleaseth but rare accidents.
> So, when this loose behavior I throw off
> And pay the debt I never promised,

> By how much better than my word I am,
> By so much shall I falsify men's hopes;
> And like bright metal on a sullen ground,
> My reformation, glittering o'er my fault,
> Shall show more goodly and attract more eyes
> Than that which hath no foil to set it off.
> I'll so offend, to make offence a skill;
> Redeeming time when men think least I will. (Act I, scene ii)

Prince Henry's soliloquy indicates the self-determination involved in sinfulness and in reformation. Our own will allows the entertainment of wickedness. Likewise, reformation comes when we combine our desire and determination to the grace and mercy of God in order to change our paths. In reforming, we become our true selves in the light of spirituality rather than the darkness of selfishness and sin.

Fortune smiles on Prince Henry as he leaves his quarters and friends in the tavern and takes his place at his father's side during a civil war threatening his father's life and his own future as king.

Many who choose to wade in the shallow waters of sinful pleasure end up drowning in the alluring deep of sin and never achieve reformation. Prince Henry is able to leave the darkness and enter into the light of his calling. Ironically, during a battle in the civil war, he kills Henry Percy, the prior envy of Henry IV, demonstrating his valor and redemption.

In the final act of *The Second Part of King Henry the Fourth*, we hear Prince Henry's passion to live according to his royal position and leave his youthful carelessness behind him. As he prepares to accept the throne following his father's death, he shares his thoughts concerning his life:

> My father is gone wild into his grave,
> For in his tomb lie my affections;
> And with his spirit sadly I survive,
> To mock the expectation of the world,
> To frustrate prophecies and to raze out
> Rotten opinion, who hath writ me down
> After my seeming. The tide of blood in me
> Hath proudly flow'd in vanity till now:
> Now doth it turn and ebb back to the sea,
> Where it shall mingle with the state of floods
> And flow henceforth in formal majesty. (Act V, scene ii)

God's grace saves us from being overcome by vanities, humiliation and loss. To enjoy the fulfillment of our destiny or calling, we, like Prince Henry, must submit ourselves to the flow of God's movement lifting us above the work-a-day world. It is never safe for us to dabble in evil or to become comfortable with sinning in any form.

Friends and environments of the past create a challenge for any person attempting to go in a new direction. Shakespeare shows us the importance of leaving these behind and, in fact, banishing any negative influences from our presence. Prince Henry leaves his former associates and surroundings behind to live honorably as King of England.

As he marches in his coronation ceremony, King Henry V is approached by his fellow and instigator in riotous living, Jack Falstaff. Falstaff expects some rewards and position from the newly crowned king; however, King Henry V has changed, and he instructs Falstaff to change also. This is the way we also must rebuff the evils of our past as they come to tempt us again. In the final act of *The Second Part of King Henry the Fourth*, King Henry V speaks directly to Falstaff:

SHAKESPEARE ON SPIRITUALITY

> I know thee not, old man: fall to thy prayers;
> How ill white hairs become a fool and jester!
> I have long dream'd of such a kind of man,
> So surfeit-swell'd, so old and so profane;
> But, being awaked, I do despise my dream.
> Make less thy body hence, and more thy grace;
> Leave gormandizing; know the grave doth gape
> For thee thrice wider than for other men.
> Reply not to me with a fool-born jest:
> Presume not that I am the thing I was;
> For God doth know, so shall the world perceive,
> That I have turn'd away my former self;
> So will I those that kept me company.
> When thou dost hear I am as I have been,
> Approach me, and thou shalt be as thou wast,
> The tutor and the feeder of my riots:
> Till then, I banish thee, on pain of death,
> As I have done the rest of my misleaders,
> Not to come near our person by ten mile. (Act V, scene v)

Reformation does not come easily. Everyday presents temptations and battles. To live the spiritually inspired life, we must forcibly turn from evil and banish it from our lives—that includes those acquaintances who would lead us where we do not want to go. King Henry V's rejection of Falstaff seems harsh and cold; however, he recognizes that he cannot risk falling back into his old way of life, so he separates himself from all corrupt parts of it. In his exhortation to Falstaff urging him to change, he exercises what today we call "tough love."

Consider the opinion of the Archbishop of Canterbury in *King Henry the Fifth* describing the reformation of King Henry V. We clearly see that it has been dramatic. We learn that the King earnestly rebukes temptations from his person as he disciplines himself to live rightly:

> The courses of his youth promised it not.
> The breath no sooner left his father's body,
> But that his wildness, mortified in him,
> Seem'd to die too; yea, at that very moment
> Consideration, like an angel, came
> And whipp'd th' offending Adam out of him,
> Leaving his body as a paradise,
> T' envelop and contain celestial spirits.
> Never was such a sudden scholar made;
> Never came reformation in a flood,
> With such a heady current, scouring faults;
> Nor never Hydra-headed wilfulness
> So soon did lose his seat, and all at once,
> As in this king. (Act I, scene i)

Shakespeare does not enjoin us to extinguish desires or to suppress passions, but through King Henry V, he shows us that our passions and desires can become subject to spirit and grace. The king describes himself in *King Henry the Fifth*,

> We are no tyrant, but a Christian king;
> Unto whose grace our passion is as subject
> As are our wretches fetter'd in our prisons: (Act I, scene ii)

So, let us not only seek to reform ourselves but also be willing to accept others who have experienced reformation. If we were all judged at our worst, none of us could gain employment or find a friend—much less a spouse. Shakespeare recommends the same in *The Two Gentlemen of Verona*. The main character Valentine has been hiding out in the forests and becomes a leader to a group of rogues banished from the city. He leads them and brings out the goodness in them. At the end of the play, he implores the Duke of Verona to pardon the whole lot of them and welcome them into city:

> These banish'd men, that I have kept withal,
> Are men endued with worthy qualities:
> Forgive them what they have committed here,
> And let them be recall'd from their exile:
> They are reformed, civil, full of good
> And fit for great employment, worthy lord. (Act V, scene iv)

None of us is without need of genuine reformation in certain areas of our lives and of acceptance from significant others. We are all experiencing or avoiding some form of reformation of the soul.

REPENTANCE OF SIN

Very similar to reformation is the concept and act of repentance. When someone repents, he or she has a change of mind and attitude concerning a habitual or singular behavior. Probably the most popular use of the word is to describe the act of turning from sin to God. Repentance is essentially a change of mind demonstrated through change of behavior. People often repent of past acts that created injury to self or others or that were just plainly wrong to do. We are human, and unfortunately, we easily slip, stumble and fall; repentance turns us back to God after our mistakes or, maybe more accurately stated, our stupidity.

Shakespeare shows several characters that repent for their actions or attitudes. Often the repentance is for evil treatment of another person. At their death, we see men repenting of what they have done. In *Hamlet*, Laertes and Hamlet each repent to one another for harms done. In contrast to showing repentance, other characters maintain their murderous hearts all the way to the end and never repent to God or to those they have wronged; these men or women, like King Richard III and the Macbeths, die with heavy, darkened hearts.

The character Henry V, who demonstrates reformation also demonstrates repentance. In *King Henry the Fifth*, prior to leading his small "band of brothers" against the larger French force, he earnestly prays to God, and in prayer recounts his acts of repentance and his current repentant heart:

> O Lord…think not upon the fault
> My father made in compassing the crown!
> I Richard's body have interred anew;
> And on it have bestow'd more contrite tears
> Than from it issued forced drops of blood:
> Five hundred poor I have in yearly pay,
> Who twice a-day their wither'd hands hold up
> Toward heaven, to pardon blood; and I have built
> Two chantries, where the sad and solemn priests
> Sing still for Richard's soul. More will I do;
> Though all that I can do is nothing worth,
> Since that my penitence comes after all,
> Imploring pardon. (Act IV, scene i)

King Henry has attempted to make recompense for his father's reckless usurpation of King Richard II's crown. He has shown renewed respect for King Richard II and has directed the focus of his administration toward humility, prayer and righteousness. His prayer reflects the essence of repentance that remains, after all, asking God for forgiveness.

The Winter's Tale is one of Shakespeare's plays that incorporates the Greek gods and their mythological interaction with humans. In the play, the god Apollo sends a message to Leontes, king of Silicia, who has experienced a severe jealous paranoia that causes discord between him and everyone close to him. Upon hearing the message from the god, Leontes quickly repents and declares a course of action proving his sincerity. He addresses Apollo regarding the people he has wronged:

> Apollo, pardon
> My great profaneness 'gainst thine oracle!
> I'll reconcile me to Polixenes,

> New woo my queen, recall the good Camillo,
> Whom I proclaim a man of truth, of mercy;
> For, being transported by my jealousies
> To bloody thoughts and to revenge, I chose
> Camillo for the minister to poison
> My friend Polixenes: which had been done,
> But that the good mind of Camillo tardied
> My swift command, though I with death and with
> Reward did threaten and encourage him,
> Not doing 't and being done: he, most humane
> And fill'd with honour, to my kingly guest
> Unclasp'd my practice, quit his fortunes here,
> Which you knew great, and to the certain hazard
> Of all incertainties himself commended,
> No richer than his honour: how he glisters
> Thorough my rust! and how his piety
> Does my deeds make the blacker! (Act III, scene ii)

When we are open to divine revelation, we may find that what we hear feels like a sword piercing our heart. The remedy to this sorrow and pain is demonstrated in the above speech—repentance and corrective action, which, when done, must be followed by accepting forgiveness and release from guilt and shame.

Another succinctly written account of true repentance is found in *As You Like It*. The acting Duke in the play, Frederick, has banished his older brother and stolen the dukedom from him. He learns that his brother has been living in the forest and has gathered a multitude of exiles that follow him. After a course of events, Frederick ventures to the forest to kill his brother and the banished multitude with him; however, a spiritual encounter saves his soul and changes the course of his life:

> Duke Frederick, hearing how that every day
> Men of great worth resorted to this forest,
> Addrest a mighty power; which were on foot,
> In his own conduct, purposely to take
> His brother here and put him to the sword:
> And to the skirts of this wild wood he came;
> Where meeting with an old religious man,
> After some question with him, was converted
> Both from his enterprise and from the world,
> His crown bequeathing to his banisht brother,
> And all their lands restored to them again
> That were with him exiled. (Act V, scene iv)

This completely describes repentance and salvation. Frederick gains salvation as evidenced by his immediate action to change his course, make amends and forfeit the profit of his wrongful acts, and he gives up the wealth, status and power of this world to gain spiritual life.

Forgiveness following repentance releases a person from endless sorrow and reparation for sin. Consider Cleomenes' counsel to Leontes in *The Winter's Tale* regarding his sincere repentance:

> Sir, you have done enough, and have perform'd
> A saint-like sorrow: no fault could you make,
> Which you have not redeem'd; indeed, paid down
> More penitence than done trespass: at the last,
> Do as the heavens have done, forget your evil;
> With them forgive yourself. (Act V, scene i)

Repentance brings us to God, and it is incomplete until we move in the right direction and receive forgiveness. Forgiveness takes away guilt and shame, so we can walk with our heads held high again. Shakespeare writes in *King Richard the Third* that a source of hope for redemption comes "By Christ's dear blood shed for our grievous sins." (Act I, scene iv). Heaven has taken such a drastic action that we may repent and receive redemption through forgiveness of sins.

Shakespeare illustrates the struggle that one endures to give up the deeds of darkness to enter into the light. Darkness can captivate those who reap its brief rewards. King Claudius provides the epitome of a man who, panged by guilt, knows he has done wrong, but he is not willing to give up the fruit of his sin:

> O, my offence is rank it smells to heaven;
> It hath the primal eldest curse upon't,
> A brother's murder! Pray can I not,
> Though inclination be as sharp as will:
> My stronger guilt defeats my strong intent;
> And, like a man to double business bound,
> I stand in pause where I shall first begin,
> And both neglect…
> But, O, what form of prayer
> Can serve my turn? 'Forgive me my foul murder'?--
> That cannot be; since I am still possest
> Of those effects for which I did the murder,--
> My crown, mine own ambition and my queen.
> May one be pardon'd and retain th' offence? (Act III, scene iii)

Claudius' attachment to the spoils of his sin is too strong to allow him to repent and give them up. He dies with his sins staid in his bosom rather than released and forgiven. Repentance sometimes requires willingness to give up something to possess peace of mind and purity of heart. Shakespeare's accounts of the rich and powerful teach that nothing gained in this world is worth losing our peace of heart and mind. So, if something you have done is causing you anxiety, guilt, shame or heartache, then repent and ask God to forgive you and to direct you in the right course.

SIN—WARNING

Anyone possessing a conscience knows the definition, the conviction, guilt, failure and shame associated with sin. Shakespeare offers commentary on the attitude of the heart and mind leading a person to sin. He shows the deceptions, errant beliefs and lust that precede sin and the earthly rewards for which people are willing to jeopardize eternity and important relationships. His plays also illustrate the consequences of sin.

Is their some treasure for which you would jeopardize your soul and the relationships that are important to you? Do you have a price on your virtue? In *Othello*, the friends Desdemona and Emilia question one another about whether they would indulge in an extra-marital affair for a certain reward:

>DESDEMONA
>Wouldst thou do such a deed for all the world?
>
>EMILIA
>The world's a huge thing: it is a great price.
>For a small vice.
>
>DESDEMONA
>In troth, I think thou wouldst not.

EMILIA
In troth, I think I should; and undo't when I had done. Marry, I would not do such a thing for a joint-ring, nor for measures of lawn, nor for gowns, petticoats, nor caps, nor any petty exhibition; but for the whole world,--why, who would not make her husband a cuckold to make him a monarch? I should venture purgatory for't.

DESDEMONA
Beshrew me, if I would do such a wrong
For the whole world.

EMILIA
Why the wrong is but a wrong i' th' world: and having the world for your labour, 'tis a wrong in your own world, and you might quickly make it right. (Act IV, scene iii)

It would be good to ask ourselves, "What would it take to make us willingly sin—if anything?" What is the reality behind the actions we would take and their consequences? We should decide before faced with the actual temptation. Emilia's argument reveals her moral relativity, while Desdemona's values are shown to be more rooted in solid principles.

In the above discourse, Shakespeare shares a common deception people fall for prior to doing acts they later regret. Emilia argues that to have an affair would be a small wrong to do in order to gain a reward, and once having the reward, she could set things right. This is comparable to thinking we can get away with stealing cookies from the cookie jar. However, deep down we know that once we have eaten the cookies we cannot return them to the cookie jar, and digested, those cookies will probably make us sick, or at the very least, make us fat and slothful. Eventually, someone, including God, will notice that the cookies are missing and that coincidentally, there is a trail of crumbs leading to us.

In *Macbeth*, prior to carrying out the act of murdering Duncan, Macbeth considers the consequences of the act. He sees that he cannot benefit from it except in title only. Macbeth weighs the pros and cons of killing the king while he is a guest at Macbeth's home:

> It were done quickly: if th' assassination
> Could trammel up the consequence, and catch,
> With his surcease, success; that but this blow
> Might be the be-all and the end-all here,
> But here, upon this bank and shoal of time,
> We'd jump the life to come. But in these cases
> We still have judgment here; that we but teach
> Bloody instructions, which, being taught, return
> To plague th' inventor: this even-handed justice
> Commends th' ingredients of our poison'd chalice
> To our own lips. He's here in double trust;
> First, as I am his kinsman and his subject,
> Strong both against the deed; then, as his host,
> Who should against his murderer shut the door,
> Not bear the knife myself. Besides, this Duncan
> Hath borne his faculties so meek, hath been
> So clear in his great office, that his virtues
> Will plead like angels, trumpet-tongued, against
> The deep damnation of his taking-off;
> And pity, like a naked new-born babe,
> Striding the blast, or heaven's cherubim, horsed

> Upon the sightless couriers of the air,
> Shall blow the horrid deed in every eye,
> That tears shall drown the wind. I have no spur
> To prick the sides of my intent, but only
> Vaulting ambition, which o'erleaps itself
> And falls on th' other. (Act I, scene vii)

Macbeth acknowledges to himself the all-around horror and stupidity of the act he is considering. The logic of his argument may have led Macbeth to abandon his murderous plans and to content himself as the king's subject; however, temptation has its helpers. Lady Macbeth serves the devil's purpose in rebuking Macbeth for his "unmanliness" and pushes him forward to do the evil deed. In the end, Macbeth is led like a beast to slaughter, his own as well as Duncan's. We should all strive to have friends around us who keep us from sin rather than lead us into sin.

After committing murder, Macbeth soon learns that sin does not reap peace or rest and that its rewards pale in comparison to its destructiveness. Even as king, he regrets his situation and the path behind and before him. He confesses to the chaotic state of his life since the murder,

> But let the frame of things disjoint, both the worlds suffer,
> Ere we will eat our meal in fear and sleep
> In the affliction of these terrible dreams
> That shake us nightly: better be with the dead,
> Whom we, to gain our peace, have sent to peace,
> Than on the torture of the mind to lie
> In restless ecstasy…
> Things bad begun make strong themselves by ill….

> I am in blood
> Stept in so far, that, should I wade no more,
> Returning were as tedious as go o'er:
> Strange things I have in head, that will to hand;
> Which must be acted ere they may be scann'd. (Act III, scenes ii&iv)

Macbeth reveals that he lives in torment because of the evil he has done to others. There may be nothing in this world as precious as personal peace, and sin destroys it. In Macbeth's course of actions, Shakespeare shows that sin leads to more and more sin rather than to something positive. Indeed, sin is a trap like quicksand in which, without repentance and rescue, the sinner will soon sink and be suffocated from all that is good. The things gained through sin do not lead to blessings. In *The Third Part of King Henry the Sixth*, Shakespeare notes, "That things ill-got have ever bad success." (Act II, scene ii)

Shakespeare knows that few people like to hear their sins repeated or to be held accountable for their sins. People often are deceived into thinking sin can be controlled or hidden while enjoyed. Invariably, in one way or another, sin is revealed to others, and it always has negative consequences—whether they are apparent or not, they exist. In *King Richard the Third*, King Richard III, who sins carelessly without remorse, pays the price in himself for each of his sins. Eventually, he faces the pangs of guilt for his atrocities:

> My conscience hath a thousand several tongues,
> And every tongue brings in a several tale,
> And every tale condemns me for a villain.
> Perjury, perjury, in the high'st degree
> Murder, stern murder, in the direst degree;

> All several sins, all used in each degree,
> Throng to the bar, crying all, 'Guilty! guilty!'
> I shall despair. There is no creature loves me;
> And if I die, no soul shall pity me:
> Nay, wherefore should they,--since that I myself
> Find in myself no pity to myself? (Act V, scene iii)

Richard III's sins bring him nothing but misery, self-hatred, and isolation. Shakespeare writes in *King Lear*, "The gods are just, and of our pleasant vices make instruments to plague us." (Act V, scene iii) Remember, spiritually you don't get away with anything. Freedom from sin's consequences comes only through repentance and receiving forgiveness.

In *Pericles*, King Antiochus has an incestuous relationship with his daughter. When Pericles discovers the affair, he confronts King Antiochus with the atrociousness of his sin, but he does not hang around to get involved; in fact, Pericles recognizes that people will go to great lengths to hide their sins:

> Great king,
> Few love to hear the sins they love to act;
> 'Twould braid yourself too near for me to tell it.
> Who has a book of all that monarchs do,
> He's more secure to keep it shut than shown:
> For vice repeated is like the wandering wind….
> By your untimely claspings with your child,
> Which pleasure fits a husband, not a father;
> And she an eater of her mother's flesh,
> By the defiling of her parent's bed;
> And both like serpents are, who though they feed
> On sweetest flowers, yet they poison breed.

> Antioch, farewell! for wisdom sees, those men
> Blush not in actions blacker than the night,
> Will shun no course to keep them from the light.
> One sin, I know, another doth provoke;
> Murder's as near to lust as flame to smoke:
> Poison and treason are the hands of sin,
> Ay, and the targets, to put off the shame:
> Then, lest my lie be cropp'd to keep you clear,
> By flight I'll shun the danger which I fear. (Act I,
>   scene i)

Shakespeare kicks this play off with a bang. Like the stories of the Bible, Shakespeare's plays lack few vices. Also like the Bible, the plays share many truths. In the passage above, we see that one sin leads to others, so it is wise to avoid those who indulge freely in any sin and to shun dangerous temptations.

Shakespeare reminds us that no person, however wise or powerful, is exempt from the consequences of his or her sin. Regarding the destruction of King Antiochus, we learn from a discussion between two lords that unforgiven sin is not overlooked by heaven. They discuss the alarming death of King Antiochus and his daughter:

> HELICANUS
> Even in the height and pride of all his glory,
> When he was seated in a chariot
> Of an inestimable value, and his daughter with him,
> A fire from heaven came, and shrivell'd up
> Their bodies, even to loathing; for they so stunk,
> That all those eyes adored them ere their fall
> Scorn now their hand should give them burial.

> ESCANES
> 'Twas very strange.
>
> HELICANUS
> And yet but justice; for though
> This king were great, his greatness was no guard
> To bar heaven's shaft, but sin had his reward. (Act II, scene iv)

Shakespeare could not say any clearer that we should do all we can to avoid sin, and when we sin, we should repent and ask God to forgive us, lest we pay for it ourselves.

God knows we are by nature tempted to sin and weak to withstand it, so God is present to help us avoid sin. Shakespeare encourages us to look to God for help:

> For every man with his affects is born,
> Not by might master'd, but by special grace:
> (*Love's Labour's Lost*--Act I, scene i)

To avoid sin, we cannot cease to be human and become dispassionate. Our passions are what give us joy and fulfillment during our lives. To master our desires by grace means we rule them rather than be ruled by them.

SPIRITUAL BATTLES

Life consists of conflicts between good and evil. We can become increasingly spiritual people and seek peace, truth and love; however, we cannot live on earth and avoid spiritual battles. We have battles within ourselves, with our environments, conflicts with individuals and with institutions. The spiritual people and Christian leaders in Shakespeare's plays engage in battles against their enemies. Evil people, such as the Macbeths, Richard III, the Goths in *Titus Andronicus* and Claudius in *Hamlet,* require that good people arise and overcome them. In *King Richard the Third*, Shakespeare explains the justification for godly men to wage war. The Earl of Richmond encourages his soldiers in their war against Richard III:

> In God's name, cheerly on, courageous friends,
> To reap the harvest of perpetual peace
> By this one bloody trial of sharp war. (Act V, scene ii)

The Earl of Richmond fights Richard III to gain peace for England. As long as evil exists, good men and women must be willing to resist it.

Shakespeare illustrates good leaders seeking God for success and help in their battles. He shows that success against enemies comes from God's hand and not man's strength alone. In *King Henry the Fifth*, King Henry is victorious in his battle against the French; however, Shakespeare provides several examples of King Henry placing his battles in God's hands before and after the victories.

Prior to the famous historical battle of Agincourt, King Henry pleads with God to strengthen his soldiers, forgive the sins of the English and grant them mercy:

> O God of battles! steel my soldiers' hearts;
> Possess them not with fear; take from them now
> The sense of reckoning, if th' opposed numbers
> Pluck their hearts from them!--Not to-day, O Lord,
> O, not to-day. (Act IV, scene i)

King Henry refers to God as the "God of battles." God involves himself in our conflicts; he stands ready to intervene on our behalf when we are on the side of good. From Shakespeare's perspective, the English are unequivocally on the side of good and God in their war against France to claim King Henry's right to the throne of France.

In *King Richard the Third,* the Earl of Richmond prepares to lead the battle to remove the murderous, usurping Richard III from the throne. His cause is in the right, and he, like Henry V, seeks God for help:

> O Thou, whose captain I account myself,
> Look on my forces with a gracious eye;
> Put in their hands Thy bruising irons of wrath,
> That they may crush down with a heavy fall
> The usurping helmets of our adversaries!
> Make us thy ministers of chastisement,
> That we may praise thee in the victory!
> To thee I do commend my watchful soul,

> Ere I let fall the windows of mine eyes:
> Sleeping and waking, O, defend me still! (Act V, scene iii)

Richmond asks God to make his soldiers instruments of God's punishment to the wicked. He also asks God to help in a dramatic fashion, so that God rather than man gains the glory from the victory.

The ghosts of several characters wronged or murdered by Richard III come during the night before the battle to visit Richard III and Richmond in their dreams. The ghosts speak curses to Richard III and blessings to Richmond. The Ghost of Buckingham's words are indicative of all the ghosts' messages and show the hand of God at work in the battle. He encourages Richmond,

> Cheer thy heart, and be thou not dismay'd:
> God and good angels fight on Richmond's side;
> And Richard falls in height of all his pride. (Act V, scene iii)

Shakespeare illustrates that God and his angels are active in the fight against evil. It is important for us not to presume God's or angels' actions on our behalf. We must double-check to make sure we are on the side of God.

The Earl of Richmond and King Henry V are victorious in their respective battles. King Henry's outnumbered army is so victorious over the French that the victory indeed could be called miraculous. King Henry's response to the news that the English have won indicates his reliance on God and his awareness and appreciation of God's intervention. He speaks of the awesome victory to his soldiers,

> Praised be God, and not our strength, for it!...
> O God, Thy arm was here;
> And not to us, but to Thy arm alone,
> Ascribe we all! When, without stratagem,
> But in plain shock and even play of battle,
> Was ever known so great and little loss
> On one part and on the other? Take it, God,
> For it is only Thine!...
> Come, go we in procession to the village.
> And be it death proclaimed through our host
> To boast of this, or take the praise from God
> Which is his only. (Act IV, scenes vii&viii)

Rather than boast and claim the glory for himself and his men, King Henry praises God and even threatens his men with death if they would boast of the victory without ascribing praise to God for it.

In *The First Part of King Henry the Sixth*, Shakespeare offers a description of Henry V's relationship to God in his battles:

> He was a king blest of the King of Kings.
> Unto the French the dreadful judgment-day
> So dreadful will not be as was his sight.
> The battles of the Lord of hosts he fought:
> The church's prayers made him so prosperous. (Act I, scene i)

According to the Bishop of Winchester's statements above, King Henry V was blessed by "the King of Kings," a reference to Jesus Christ, as he fought God's battles, and the Bishop assigns credit to God for victories in response to the church's prayers.

Shakespeare demonstrates in these examples a doubtless

belief in the presence and involvement of God in the battles of people. Our responsibility is to believe that God would actually help us in our day-to-day conflicts and challenges. Our conflicts may seem minuscule and not even significant enough to appear on the radar screen of God's agenda; however, the opposite is true. If we humble ourselves and pray for God's help, we can expect him to respond to the smallest and largest concerns we have. Then we can face our troubles and say as King Henry V does in regard to his enemies, "We are in God's hand, brother, not in theirs." (*King Henry the Fifth*--Act III, scene vi)

STEALING RELIGION

Religion is not synonymous to spirituality. Religion describes processes, organizations, activities, and rules created for spiritual purposes, but religion does not always remain true to the purposes for which it is created. You can probably think of examples of religious people who seem to lack all measure of spirituality as evidenced by lack of virtues such as love, joy, peace, mercy, grace, generosity, cheerfulness, etc. Although, pure and sincere religions serve as stepping stones to intimacy with God, Shakespeare's plays confirm that religious people are not necessarily spiritual or holy.

Some religious people use religion to serve their own selfish desires; they are wolves in sheep's clothing. Shakespeare does not disguise his disdain of these characters in his plays. His characterizations of the religious leaders whose primary concerns are their own status, power and position are strong indictments against those who make selfish use of religion while manipulating peoples' desires to please God. These religious types are not distinguishable in behavior from typical politicians in the plays; both seek power and treasure.

Those characters using religion for personal gain face consequences for their duplicity. Cardinal Beaufort, great uncle to King Henry VI, rarely seems concerned with spirituality. The Duke of Gloster rebukes him in *The First Part of King Henry the Sixth* for his blatant hypocrisy:

> Name not religion, for thou lovest the flesh;
> And ne'er throughout the year to church thou go'st,
> Except it be to pray against thy foes. (Act I, scene i)

The Duke of Gloster later calls the Cardinal a "wolf in sheep's array." (Act I, scene iii) In *The First and Second Parts of King Henry the Sixth*, we learn not only that the Cardinal accepts sums of money to place people in religious positions but also conspires to murder the king. In *The First Part of King Henry the Sixth,* while alone, he proclaims his ambition:

> Now Winchester will not submit, I trow,
> Or be inferior to the proudest peer.
> Humphrey of Gloster, thou shalt well perceive
> That, neither in birth or for authority,
> The bishop will be overborne by thee:
> I'll either make thee stoop and bend thy knee,
> Or sack this country with a mutiny. (Act V, scene i)

This is not a particularly spiritual quest that the Cardinal has in mind. Following his taking part in the murder of the Duke of Gloster, the Cardinal is taken by a "sudden grievous sickness" and dies. He is never able to enjoy the prize of power for which he labored. His crimes and wickedness show how far even a religious person can fall when he or she becomes consumed with lust, greed and selfish ambition.

In *The Second Part of King Henry the Fourth*, the Archbishop of York seeks personal advantage and gain from King Richard II's death. He uses his religious position to stir up followers who will help him overthrow King Henry IV. One of the king's followers describes the Archbishop's perverted use of religion:

> But now the bishop
> Turns insurrection to religion:
> Supposed sincere and holy in his thoughts,
> He's followed both with body and with mind;
> And doth enlarge his rising with the blood
> Of fair King Richard, scraped from Pomfret stones;
> Derives from heaven his quarrel and his cause;
> Tells them he doth bestride a bleeding land,
> Gasping for life under great Bolingbroke [King Henry IV];
> And more and less do flock to follow him. (Act I, scene i)

How many people over the ages have been manipulated by selfish people like the Archbishop of York using religion as a means to control?

In *The Merchant of Venice*, Shakespeare sums up the character of those using religion for selfish purposes:

> The devil can cite Scripture for his purpose.
> An evil soul, producing holy witness,
> Is like a villain with a smiling cheek,
> A goodly apple rotten at the heart:
> O, what a goodly outside falsehood hath! (Act I, scene iii)

Scriptures can be a tool in the hands of the righteous and the evil. A wide smile and a gleam in the eye do not translate into a pure and noble heart.

Queen Katherine in *King Henry the Eighth* possesses a skeptical and healthy caution concerning men of the cloth.

When approached by Cardinal Wolsey and Cardinal Capeius, she tells the king:

> I do not like their coming. Now I think on't,
> They should be good men; their affairs as righteous:
> But all hoods make not monks. (Act III, scene i)

Not all who claim to be religious leaders actually lead people to God, regardless of appearances and titles.

King Richard III demonstrates how to wear the mantel of religion when trying to deceive honorable people:

> with a piece of Scripture,
> Tell them that God bids us do good for evil:
> And thus I clothe my naked villany
> With old odd ends stoln out of holy writ;
> And seem a saint, when most I play the devil. (Act I, scene iii)

Some people have a difficult time imagining that a religious person could actually be evil. Shakespeare, however, possesses a keen understanding of evil and of what evil people desire. Nothing could benefit a hungry wolf more than possessing the appearance of a lamb. He tells us in *Love's Labour's Lost*, "Devils soonest tempt, resembling spirits of light." (Act IV, scene iii)

In *King Henry the Eighth*, King Henry VIII learns that Cardinal Wolsey has been stockpiling riches for his own benefit. The king dislodges the Cardinal of his position in the state and subjects him to humiliation and loss. The Cardinal accepts the rebuke from the King as God's correction. He repents of his worldliness and resigns himself to heaven. To

Cromwell, he remorsefully confesses the selfish use he has made of his religious position and gives him advice based on the lessons he has learned from his downfall:

> Mark but my fall, and that that ruin'd me.
> Cromwell, I charge thee, fling away ambition:
> By that sin fell the angels; how can man, then,
> The image of his Maker, hope to win by it?
> Love thyself last: cherish those hearts that hate thee;
> Corruption wins not more than honesty.
> Still in thy right hand carry gentle peace,
> To silence envious tongues. Be just, and fear not:
> Let all the ends thou aim'st at be thy country's,
> Thy God's, and truth's; then if thou fall'st, O Cromwell,
> Thou fall'st a blessed martyr! Serve the king;
> And,--prithee, lead me in:
> There take an inventory of all I have,
> To the last penny; 'tis the king's: my robe,
> And my integrity to heaven, is all
> I dare now call mine own. O Cromwell, Cromwell!
> Had I but served my God with half the zeal
> I served my king, he would not in mine age
> Have left me naked to mine enemies. (Act III, scene ii)

Serving God is not easy. Men and women pursuing spiritual vocations contend with all the temptations of the world just as others do. No automatic means to becoming spiritual and immune to the temptations of power, wealth and status exists for us.

If there is a spiritual leader in your life, there is no greater service you could provide them than praying for their steadfastness in service to God. According to Shakespeare, religious leaders should resolve themselves to have the attitude that Cardinal Wolsey regains following his fall from King Henry VIII's graces: "Farewell the hopes of court! My hopes in heaven do dwell." (Act III, scene ii)

VANITY, VANITY

Each of us possesses our own standard for measuring the value of things in this world and in the world to come. Some people place higher value on material possessions while others place more importance on intangible things such as relationships and peace. We invest our time and energies to gain the things we value most highly. Shakespeare's plays involve struggles over riches, power, status, land, nations, love and pride. Through the outcomes in his plays and his words, Shakespeare addresses the concept of vanity. His plays instruct us how to live meaningful, full lives that gain eternal rewards without neglecting worldly needs and good works.

Shakespeare displays one of the most poignant examples of vanity by summarizing the fortune of Henry V's gains from France and Henry VI's subsequent losses to France. King Henry V wins France's throne for England; sadly, he dies prematurely and leaves a young son, King Henry VI, to reign over both kingdoms. His reign is characterized by conflicts and striving among his uncles and others who also want the throne. His own indifference to the plight of the state contributes to it ending with his murder, a civil war, and France regaining all it had lost to his father.

In *King Henry the Fifth,* Shakespeare describes the vanity of King Henry V's triumphantly gaining a nation soon lost by the next generation:

> Small time, but in that small most greatly liv'd
> This star of England: Fortune made his sword;
> By which the world's best garden he achieved,
> And of it left his son imperial lord.
> Henry the Sixth, in infant bands crown'd King
> Of France and England, did this king succeed;
> Whose state so many had the managing,
> That they lost France and made his England bleed:
>   (Epilogue)

All of the lives lost in the battles the English fought against France to win Henry V the throne of France are, over time, proven to have been lost in vain.

All the riches that we can gain in this world shall be left in it. Shakespeare describes the journey in *Measure for Measure*:

> If thou art rich, thou'rt poor;
> For, like an ass whose back with ingots bows,
> Thou bear's thy heavy riches but a journey,
> And death unloads thee. (Act III, scene i)

We do not always have the luxury in the world to choose what burdens we bear. We can determine to avoid taking on extra burdens that will serve us little but weigh us down physically and spiritually. The riches we have in this life should serve to bless us and others—to bring joy not burdens.

In *Macbeth*, Macbeth bargains everything to gain the crown. The witches' prediction that Banquo's sons and not his own will be kings after him maddens him. He laments his vanity in giving up all he had enjoyed for a throne that brings him no lasting peace or heritage:

> No son of mine succeeding. If 't be so,
> For Banquo's issue have I filed my mind;
> For them the gracious Duncan have I murder'd;
> Put rancours in the vessel of my peace
> Only for them; and mine eternal jewel
> Given to the common enemy of man,
> To make them kings, the seed of Banquo kings! (Act III, scene i)

Macbeth verbalizes his loss of his soul to the devil in exchange for the throne: his "eternal jewel" to the "common enemy of man." Shakespeare describes a man who has sold his soul to the devil for an illusory position of power and majesty.

In the process, Macbeth loses all that is truly valuable in this world and in eternity: his relationships with others, his soul, his peace and even his days on earth. Lady Macbeth's guilt drives her to mental illness and suicide. Macbeth is so consumed with maintaining his throne that he cannot even offer attention to his wife or sympathy at her death. When told of her death, he turns to self-pity and describes the vanity of the life lived for selfish gain:

> She should have died hereafter;
> There would have been a time for such a word.--
> To-morrow, and to-morrow, and to-morrow,
> Creeps in this petty pace from day to day
> To the last syllable of recorded time,
> And all our yesterdays have lighted fools
> The way to dusty death. Out, out, brief candle!
> Life's but a walking shadow, a poor player
> That struts and frets his hour upon the stage
> And then is heard no more: it is a tale

Told by an idiot, full of sound and fury,
Signifying nothing. (Act V, scene iv)

    In the above words, Shakespeare poignantly summarizes the experience and result of living selfishly. The life lived generously and humbly creates a different outcome and perspective. The spiritually minded person tries to keep an eye on eternity to prevent consumption and deception by the pleasures of this world. The generous, caring person's life has meaning, while the selfishly ambitious person invariably lives a life "signifying nothing."

    God's grace empowers people to seek spiritual rewards that can never be lost. In *King Henry the Eighth*, Cardinal Wolsey becomes consumed with seeking power, wealth and status. After his lechery is discovered and punished by King Henry VIII, the Cardinal repents of his selfishness, and before dying, he shares his newfound insights regarding worthwhile actions versus vain actions:

> So farewell to the little good you bear me.
> Farewell! a long farewell, to all my greatness!
> This is the state of man: to-day he puts forth
> The tender leaves of hopes; to-morrow blossoms,
> And bears his blushing honours thick upon him;
> The third day comes a frost, a killing frost,
> And, when he thinks, good easy man, full surely
> His greatness is a-ripening,--nips his root,
> And then he falls, as I do. I have ventured,
> Like little wanton boys that swim on bladders,
> This many summers in a sea of glory,
> But far beyond my depth: my high-blown pride
> At length broke under me and now has left me,

> Weary and old with service, to the mercy
> Of a rude stream, that must for ever hide me.
> Vain pomp and glory of this world, I hate ye:
> I feel my heart new open'd. O, how wretched
> Is that poor man that hangs on princes' favours!
> There is, betwixt that smile we would aspire to,
> That sweet aspect of princes, and their ruin,
> More pangs and fears than wars or women have:
> And when he falls, he falls like Lucifer,
> Never to hope again. (Act III, scene ii)

In the final words of this repentant man, Shakespeare delivers the core lessons of vanity. His words inspire me, and I hope you, to consider the value of life and its pursuits. The Cardinal strives for material gain and the approval of others in this world, and he ends up losing everything. Our lives must be built on a foundation that cannot so easily be removed, destroyed or disparaged. It must be an eternal foundation of substance.

VIRTUE OF VIRTUES

True spirituality leads to a virtuous life lived with a pure, loving and humble heart. Virtuous people glow and touch those around them with a spark of the divine. In *Macbeth*, Shakespeare describes virtues as the following "king-becoming graces:"

> As justice, verity, temperance, stableness,
> Bounty, perseverance, mercy, lowliness,
> Devotion, patience, courage, fortitude. (Act IV, scene iii)

These virtues are not ambiguous characteristics a person is born with or without. A person chooses to live according to these graces or to live otherwise.

In *Macbeth*, the King of England possesses such virtue that blessings and healing flow from him to the sick and diseased people that come to him for prayers. Malcolm describes the king's grace:

> A most miraculous work in this good king;
> Which often, since my here-remain in England,
> I have seen him do. How he solicits heaven,
> Himself best knows: but strangely-visited people,
> All swoln and ulcerous, pitiful to the eye,
> The mere despair of surgery, he cures,
> Hanging a golden stamp about their necks,

> Put on with holy prayers: and 'tis spoken,
> To the succeeding royalty he leaves
> The healing benediction. With this strange virtue,
> He hath a heavenly gift of prophecy,
> And sundry blessings hang about his throne,
> That speak him full of grace. (Act IV, scene iii)

A person gains virtue at the sacrifice of many temporal pleasures and indulgences throughout life. Shakespeare shows that virtue brings rewards and blessings that not all the riches in the world can buy. Virtuous people experience abundantly satisfying lives, and throughout their lives, they share blessings with others.

Shakespeare confirms the great value of virtue in *Pericles*:

> I hold it ever,
> Virtue and cunning were endowments greater
> Than nobleness and riches: careless heirs
> May the two latter darken and expend;
> But immortality attends the former.
> Making a man a god. (Act III, scene ii)

The things that we often want so badly tie us to the earth, creating burdens rather than relieving them. However, when we gain the qualities associated with spiritual pursuits, we become most godlike and tied more to heaven than to earth.

Unfortunately, people tend to emphasize a person's faults rather than virtues. Shakespeare explains that, "Men's evil manners live in brass, their virtues we write in water." (*King Henry the Eighth*--Act IV, scene ii) Shakespeare encourages us to believe in virtue in ourselves and in others. Praising another's virtues helps those virtues to grow.

A character like Macbeth can cause us never to feel comfortable trusting a seemingly virtuous man again. In the play, Malcolm objects to such an attitude by comparing the appearances of angels to the appearances of virtuous men:

> Angels are bright still, though the brightest fell;
> Though all things foul would wear the brows of grace,
> Yet grace must still look so. (Act IV, scene iii)

Malcolm explains that although Satan, the brightest angel, proved disloyal, many angels obediently kept their places of service to God and continue to shine his bright light. Likewise, although deceitful people can fool us, people who are truly good, honest, and sincere exist in more abundance than the duplicitous. To live a fulfilling and spiritual life, we require satisfying relationships with people we trust. As we seek to be virtuous, we can trust that God will bring like-minded people into our paths to join us on our journey.

A virtuous life does not imply withdrawal from others, timidity or passivity. To the contrary, "Virtue is bold, and goodness never fearful." (*Measure for Measure*--Act III, scene i) Therefore, live boldly as you courageously pursue spiritual treasures and accomplish earthly good.

Made in the USA
Columbia, SC
21 July 2021

42189033R00115